The Plight of a Sorcerer

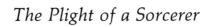

The Plight of a Sorcerer

Georges Dumézil

Edited by
Jaan Puhvel and David Weeks

UNIVERSITY OF CALIFORNIA PRESS
Berkeley Los Angeles London

University of California Press
Berkeley and Los Angeles, California

University of California Press, Ltd.
London, England

Library of Congress Cataloging in Publication Data

Dumézil, Georges, 1898–
The plight of a sorcerer.

Translation of: Entre les dieux et les démos—un sorcier (Kāvya Uśanas, Kavi Usan), which is pt. 2 of v. 2, Types épiques indo-européens—un héros, un sorcier, un roi, of Mythe et épopée.
Continues: The stakes of the warrior. c1983.
Continued by: The destiny of a king. 1973.
Includes bibliographies.
1. Mythology, Iranian. 2. Mythology, Indic. 3. Demonology. I. Puhvel, Jaan. II. Weeks, David. III. Dumézil, Georges, 1898– . Mythe et épopée. 2. Types épiques indo-européens—un héros, un sorcier, un roi. 2. Plight of a sorcerer. IV. Title.
BL1525.D8613 1986 299'.15 86-6924
ISBN 0-520-05534-9 (alk. paper)

Printed in the United States of America

1 2 3 4 5 6 7 8 9

Contents

Editors' Preface

Volume II (1971) of Georges Dumézil's three-volume *Mythe et épopée* (1968, 1971, 1973) was subtitled "Types épiques indo-européens: un héros, un sorcier, un roi." The three parts were sufficiently self-contained to warrant consideration as individual monographs, and such has been the shape of their transposition to Anglo-American vernacular and bibliopoly. The third and last part appeared as *The Destiny of a King* (University of Chicago Press, 1973), being a seminal study of the nature of the king's station in early Indo-European society from India to Ireland. It dealt especially with the validation, reinforcement, or restoration of kingship by virginal female figures, or the king's daughter and her miraculous son(s), and conversely with the threat that the king's own sons tended to pose to the king's well-being. The initial third was published as *The Stakes of the Warrior* (University of California Press, 1983), detailing and comparing the careers of a Norse, an Indic, and a Greek type-hero as champions of regal worth on the one hand, and yet as tragically flawed and spiritually sundered victims of antagonisms between rival divine forces on the other.

The middle third, contained in the book at hand, bore the heading "Entre les dieux et les démons: un sorcier (Kāvya Uśanas, Kavi Usan)." From an Indo-European standpoint its range would seem more restrictive. Despite occasional references to Celtic, Greek, or Norse material, the sights are firmly set on Indo-Iranian as a binary focus of reconstruction. This very concentration confers on the study a power of penetration which serves to enhance the comparativistic aspects. Far from chasing down further tripartitions or piling up additional data on trifunctionality (as his detractors are invariably prone to suspect), Dumézil poses and answers two very basic questions of Indic and Iranian studies. His success in doing so vindicates the judicious use of the comparative method in solving not only superstructural equations but also in gaining new insights into rectilineal developments within individual cultures.

The first question is the very viability and extent of the mythological concept "Indo-Iranian." Linguistically it has made as much sense, from the beginnings of modern scholarship, as would any other close-knit dialect area. The language of the oldest *ṚgVeda* and that of Zarathuštra's *Gāthās* are no more divergent from each other than, for example, modern Italian and Spanish as outcomes of Latin. The formal and substantive contents point at every step to rather recent joint origins. And yet, rebounding from the excesses of nineteenth-century comparative mythology, most of the leading Indic, Iranian, and Indo-Iranian scholars of the early twentieth century would have no dealings with extralinguistic comparativism. Gradually the obvious close similarities of Vedic and pre- and preter-Zoroastrian Iranian religion penetrated the self-imposed blinders of scholarship, but such consideration had not been seriously revived for the post-Vedic and later Iranian epic traditions. Dumézil's task is to show that epic, no less than pantheonic, figures are amenable to cogent comparison in terms of Indo-Iranian prototypes. He demonstrates this in depth by the example of Kāvya Uśanas, known allusively in the Vedas and extensively in the *Mahābhārata* as the resident wizard of the demons, comparing him to his near namesake Kavi Usan (Kay Ūs, Kaūs) of Iranian record (from the *Avesta* to the *Book of Kings*), the best-known king of the legendary Kayanid dynasty, who is also in shifting and uneasy league with demons. Powers of life restoration and age manipulation are but a few of the many specific and peculiar common traits of the two figures, leading to the postulation of a proto-Indo-Iranian sorcerer type connected with the title *kaví* ("seer, sage" in Sanskrit), a priestly freelance magician readily absorbed into the brahmin class in India (Bṛhaspati or Brahmaṇaspati being Kāvya Uśanas's opposite number in the gods' camp) but somehow showing up as a special component in the Iranian king list, following the mythical Pishdadians but antedating the more nearly historical period.

Such transposition may have to do with the Zoroastrian upheaval, which not only demonized patron deities of the warrior class but perhaps extended the halo of rulership to priestly manipulators (witness the recent Iranian parallel of 1979). But whatever the mechanism, it makes it clear that the Kayanids, far from being the historical dynasty postulated by most eminent one-track Iranianists, are in fact mythical creatures fabricated from Indo-Iranian (and possibly ultimately Indo-European) cloth. This is a conclusion of immense significance for the study of Iranian antiquity and a notable illustration of how cogent comparativistic induction can deductively reverberate in the separate component parts of the comparison.

Our editorial task has consisted of revising and making uniform the contributions of the translators, in order to ensure stylistic consistency and continuity and preserve some measure of the author's individual manner of writing. A complicating factor has been Dumézil's liberal use of sometimes lengthy direct quotations from primary and secondary sources in many languages. For his renderings of the *Mahābhārata* we have whenever possible (Books I–V) substituted the English version by J. A. B. van Buitenen (Chicago, 1973–1978); passages lacking in the Poona edition or in van Buitenen have been translated directly from the Sanskrit. For the Iranian material in Persian and Arabic Dumézil has for the most part used such standard French renderings as Jules Mohl's for Firdausi and Hermann Zotenberg's for Tabarī and al-Thaʿālibī; here the unavailability of any comparable English standard has made us rely on the French versions (for Firdausi, however, the versified English version of A. G. Warner and E. Warner [London, 1905] has also been consulted and compared). For the *Dēnkart* and the *Bundahišn* Dumézil relies on the Madan and Anklesaria editions, with translations sometimes supplied (and, in the latter case, emended) by Jean-Pierre de Menasce; our renderings take into account the various versions, but above all the text of the original. For the Irish and Welsh passages in chapter 4 we were able to use very up-to-date translations by Elizabeth A. Gray and Patrick K. Ford.

In quoting modern scholarly literature in English or German Dumézil is inconsistent: Mary Boyce is quoted in English in the Introduction, but Ilya Gershevitch is quoted in French translation or paraphrase in chapter 3. Albert Debrunner is quoted in German, but Friedrich von Spiegel and Herman Lommel are quoted in French translation in chapter 1. We have translated all quoted passages from original French (such as Arthur Christensen), used the originals for passages from English, and rendered all German quotations directly from the originals.

Introduction

The material of the following study has taken shape at the confluence of two lines of inquiry: one comparative and Indo-Iranian, aimed at observing and pinning down a legendary figure presumed to be common to the ancestors of the Indians and the Iranians; the other historical and Iranian, seeking to test the generally accepted documentary value of an important piece of tradition about pre-Achaemenid Iran.

The comparison of the ideologies of India and Iran, undertaken some time ago and now having progressed quite far, lately is faced with a paradox. Although, in spite of the originality and vigor of Zoroastrian reform, we can see with precision the system of gods, quite a few myths, many rituals, the types of priests, and even the conceptions of social structure of the Indo-Iranians before their division, still we remain in uncertainty, when not in total darkness, when we attempt to apply the same comparative methods to heroes and their legends.

The best cases are mixed ones in which Iran seems to have historicized, if not a god, at least a superman—unless it is India that has more or less mythicized a hero. Two of these are well known and clearly show the limits of what can be obtained by comparison. These are figures who are in the *Avesta* the king Yima and the champion Θraētaona, and who will be in the epic tradition the two kings Jamšid and Feridūn. Iran, but not India, has made them closely connected, the second avenging the sad death of the first. Yima has been treated in *The Destiny of a King* (University of Chicago Press, 1973); here let us limit ourselves to a quick survey of the dossier of Θraētaona.

Θraētaona is first and foremost the killer of the three-headed dragon, Aži Dahāka. His name is derived from *ϑrita*, literally "third." In the *ṚgVeda*, the killer of the tricephalous monster is generally Indra, but he is sometimes assisted by a figure named Trita, and sometimes the deed is attributed to Trita alone, "inspired by Indra."[1] Trita is conceived of at some times as a man above mankind, at others as a kind of daimon. True to his name, he is the third of three brothers, the elder two of whom, following a common folkloric pattern, are not his equals, are jealous of him, and try to kill him; one Vedic hymn, elucidated by an *itihāsa* which can be found even in the *Mahābhārata*, clearly alludes to this unpleasant episode. Θraētaona likewise has two brothers and at least in the epic version is the target of their envy and their ambushes. Thus we are faced here with shared material, almost mythical in India and nearly secular in the *Avesta*, and transformed into history in the texts of the Islamic period, in which Feridūn has taken his place in the sequence of Iranian kings as the successor of the three-headed usurper, Zohāk.

What complicates matters while at the same time enriching the comparison is that Θrita is also attested in Iran, distinct from Θraētaona, with a much reduced but important role: in the *Avesta* he is the first healer; commissioned by Ahura Mazdā, he gathered herbs and concocted remedies against the myriad diseases created by Aŋra Mainyu.[2] Something of this function is found in Θraētaona as well, because a middle Iranian text, the *Dēnkart*, in a summary of a lost portion of the Avestan compilation, attributes medicine, among other activities, to Frētōn,[3] and because some

[1] *The Destiny of the Warrior* (Chicago, 1970), pp. 12–28.

[2] Ibid., p. 26f. (*Vidēvdāt* 20.1–4).

[3] Ibid. p. 18 (*Dēnkart*, ed. Dhanjishah Meherjibhai Madan [Bombay, 1911], 7.2.27; Marijan Molé, *La légende de Zoroastre selon les textes pehlevis*, 1967, p. 8). On the *Dēnkart*, see Jean-Pierre de Menasce, *Une encyclopédie mazdéenne, le Dēnkart* (Conférences R. Katrak), *Bibl. de l'École des Hautes Études, Sciences Religieuses*, vol. LXIX (1958).

writers of the Islamic period still knew that this art went back to Feridūn (Afridun, etc.); thus Belʿamī:[4]

> Afridun held the kingship for two hundred years after Kaveh's death, and he governed the world with fairness and justice. The magi say that this prince was a worshipper of fire. He was the first to study astronomy; he composed the Kharesmian tablets and he was the founder of the science of medicine. He was also the first king who rode an elephant.

The mythical Trita of the Vedas, in connection with his participation in the killing of the Tricephalus, has a similar function: in rituals, he takes upon himself, with all its consequences, the taint resulting from necessary murders, especially sacrificial killings, and diffuses it through a series of intermediaries so that neither the original killer nor he himself suffers any ill effects;[5] thus he is successively scapegoat and purifier. By extension, and this already in a hymn of the *ṚgVeda*, he is invoked to repel nightmares and the nocturnal onslaughts of evil spirits in general.[6]

Thus the same function is firmly established, still mythical in India, humanized in Iran: while the daimon Trita, unseen, destroys ritual or moral stain by mysterious means, Θrita is already an herbalist and Feridūn founds the "science" of medicine.

The comparison can hardly be pushed further. The essential fact remains that the Indian Trita has never descended to the historical level, while Θraētaona has gradually done so, to the point where he furnishes one of the most illustrious figures for the initial segment of the *Book of Kings*.

Nonetheless Trita–Θraētaona, with Yama–Yima, is the only case where the agreement in name is incontestably supported by some substantive accordances in the stories. Others that seemed promising at first have turned out to be deceptive. Such is the case

[4] Chap. 43 (Hermann Zotenberg, trans., *Chronique de Abou Djafar Mohammed ben Djarir ben Yezid Tabarī, traduite sur la version persane d'Abou Ali Mohammed Belʿamī* . . . [Paris, 1958], I: 119).

[5] *The Destiny of the Warrior*, p. 25f.

[6] Ibid., p. 26f. (*ṚgVeda* 8.47).

with the "hero with the gaunt horse," Sanskrit Kṛśāśva, Avestan Kərəsāspa.

Kərəsāspa is one of Iran's most conspicuous characters, both in the *Avesta* and, in the forms Karsāsp, Garšāsp, and so on, in the Pahlavi texts and the Persian epic. He performs exploits, listed in the sources, at least one of which confronts him with a superhuman, monstrous enemy, Gandarəwa, who is well known in India (Vedic *gandharvá*). He is not a king of Iran, save in late transformations of the tradition, and Wikander has greatly advanced the study by underlining Kərəsāspa's cultic relationships with the god Vayu in Iran itself, as well as the kinship of his type with that of the Indic Bhīma, the second of the Pāṇḍavas and the brutal son of the god Vāyu: both prefer to arm themselves with a club, both imprudently throw in with female demons, both are intemperate, sinning by their blind violence and thereby getting themselves into difficult situations, and so on.[7]

But Bhīma is not the same as Kṛśāśva, this hero Kṛśāśva who nevertheless did exist and who was important, to judge by the terms used by the epics in what little they say of him. Between him and Kərəsāspa only one correspondence has been found, one as thin as the unknown horse must have been which he carries in his name. Expanding on a suggestion made by one of the most insightful and level-headed of the early comparativists, Friedrich von Spiegel, and repeated as well by James Darmesteter, Marijan Molé has defined very well what the two heroes have in common.[8] His analysis is summarized here.

In the beginning of the *Rāmāyaṇa*, the ascetic Viśvāmitra has just asked king Daśaratha to entrust to him his young son Rāma—

[7] "Pāṇḍavasagan och Mahābhāratas mytiska förutsättningar," *Religion och Bibel* VI (1947): 27–39, especially p. 34.

[8] "Deux notes sur le Rāmāyaṇa," *Collection Latomus* XLV (=*Hommages à Georges Dumézil*, 1960), I: "L'initiation guerrière de Rāma et celle de Rustam." In *Die arische Periode und ihre Zustände* (1887), p. 264, Friedrich von Spiegel had remarked that in both the *Viṣṇu Purāṇa* and the *Rāmāyaṇa*, Kṛśāśva is the spouse of two "victories," Jayā and Vijayā, the daughters of Prajāpati, with whom he fathered the *śastradevatāḥ*, the "weapon divinities," one hundred in all (fifty by each of his wives).

the incarnate Viṣṇu—saying that he is the only one who can exterminate the Rākṣasa demons, who, dangerously, also have been incarnated; he will prepare him for his role, but Rāma must stay with Viśvāmitra for the ten nights set for a sacrifice, or victory over the monsters will be impossible. As Daśaratha is hesitant, the ascetic assures him that there is no risk in the undertaking because he himself will give Rāma extraordinary weapons:[9]

> *sarvāstrāṇi kṛśāśvasya putrāḥ paramadharmikāḥ*
> *kauśikāya purā dattā yadā rājyaṁ praśasati*
> *te 'pi putrāḥ krśāśvasya prajāpatisutāsutāḥ*
> *naikarūpā mahāvīrya dīptimanto jayāvahāḥ*

> ". . . all the weapons, Kṛśāśva's sons of highest virtue,
> long ago given to Kauśika when he held the kingship.
> These sons of Kṛśaśva, born of Prajāpati's daughters,
> multi-formed, flashing victory-bringers of great virtue."

Daśaratha gives in, and Rāma goes with his master to his hermitage. There, after numerous digressions, and in particular after Rāma has killed the monster Tāṭakā, Viśvāmitra at last gives him the promised weapons, reiterating to him that they are "the sons of Kṛśāśva":[10]

> *kṛśāśvatanayān rāma bhāsvarān kāmarūpinaḥ*
> *pratīccha mama bhadraṁ te pātrabhūto 'si rāghava*

> "Kṛśāśva's shining sons, Rāma, which take any desired form,
> Receive them from me; blessings upon you; a worthy recipient
> you are, Rāghava."

In the Iranian *Shāh Nāmeh*, the theme is found in the course of the "childhood" of a particularly important hero, Rustam.

> Once more [writes Marijan Molé[11]] Iran is invaded by Afrāsyāb [Avestan Fraŋrasyan], and, after the death of Sām, there is no one who can defend it. The grandees retreat into Zābulistan, to Zāl: there they find a knight [Rustam, son of

[9] *Rāmāyaṇa* 1.21.13–14.
[10] Ibid., 1.27.10.

Zāl and grandson of Sām] who will be able to fight their enemies, and who already has to his credit such exploits as the conquest of Spand and the killing of the raging elephant, but who has not yet confronted as formidable an adversary as Afrāsyāb. Zāl considers his son's youth and inexperience, and hesitates before allowing him to get involved. But Rustam does not feel the same doubts as his father and has no fear of confronting the Turanian king: war is his business, he is ill at ease amidst festivals and banquets; what he asks above all is a mighty steed to carry him into the thick of battle, and weapons to go with it. In the end Zāl declares himself convinced. The hero will choose his mount as soon as may be. For the moment, he has proposed for him a weapon worthy of him (*Shāh Nāmeh*, ed. Vullers-Naficy, I, p. 282):[12]

> "You who are weary of resting and wine-cups, I shall bring you the club of Sām the knight, which I keep as a remembrance of him in the world, and with which you killed the raging elephant. May you live forever, O Pahlevan!"

And he takes it:[13]

> He ordered them to bring this club of Sām, which had served him in the war of the Māzandarān, (which was brought) to the glorious Pahlevan that he might exterminate his enemies with it. It was an inheritance that, from the illustrious Garšāsp, had come down from father to son to the knight Sām.[14] Rustam, when he saw his grandfather's weapon, smiled with his two lips and rejoiced.

The club with which Sām had led the war in the Māzandarān ensures victory thanks to the powers inherent in it. Sām had gotten this weapon from his forefathers the Narīmān, the

[11] Art. cit. in footnote 8, pp. 142–145; *Le Livre des Rois* I, ed. and trans. Jules Mohl (Paris, 1838), pp. 442–446 (trans. pp. 443–447, in section 10, "Guershasp"). These lines are not found in the Russian critical edition, E. Bertel's' *Firdousi Šāx-nāme, kritičeskij tekst*, 9 vols. (Moscow, 1966–1971); the episode is in II: 52.

[12] Verses 82–83 (Mohl, p. 447).

[13] Verses 84–87 (ibid.).

[14] *zi garšāsp i yal mānd-a bud yādgār*
pidar tā pidar tā bi sām i savār

Karīms,[15] and God knows who else, ancestors who got it from Garšāsp.

Despite differences in shading and certain details that can be explained by the fact that the two stories are inserted into completely different contexts, their general structure is similar.

The young hero is at the beginning of his career, and has to take part in a great battle. Rustam will save Iran from the Turanian invasion; Rāma will wipe out the Rākṣasas. When he receives for good the weapons of Kərəsāspa/Kṛśāśva, the hero already has a first deed to his credit: the slaying of Tāṭakā, and the killing of the white elephant plus the conquest of the fortress of Spand. Henceforth, the arms will be with him until his death. He is not the first to use them; these weapons have already allowed Kauśika to ensure his sovereignty, and Sām to exterminate the Sagsās in the Māzandarān. There is one important difference: Kṛśāśva is not an ancestor of Rāma as Sām is of Rustam. This feature is explained by the evolution of the Iranian epic and particularly the Sistanian saga.

Thus the result of this detailed study comes down to this: the only ancient personal datum about Kṛśāśva that survives in India is that he was once the possessor, or even the "father," of miraculous weapons—the club which is a mark of Kərəsāspa is not explicitly mentioned—which, passed down via intermediaries and generations, serve to outfit a young hero for a very important deed. Of Kṛśāśva's story itself nothing has survived.

It was natural, by applying the same method, to investigate the only other case exactly parallel to that of Kərəsāspa and Kṛśāśva, but it was more troublesome because the Vedic texts, and already the *ṚgVeda*, are involved in it: namely, the case of the Iranian king Kavi Usa(δa)n and the Indic magician Kāvya (or kavi) Uśanas, which Friedrich von Spiegel, in his writings of 1871 and 1887,

[15] M. Dj. Moinfar, referring to his *Vocabulaire arabe dans le Livre des Rois de Firdousi* (Wiesbaden, 1970), p. 41, points out to me that the word *karīm-ān* is the plural of Arabic *karīm*, "generous," and that it has been wrongly taken as a proper name, designating the father of Narīmān, in the Russian edition (index), Molé's article, and others.

had likewise dealt with immediately after that of Kərəsāspa and Kṛśāśva.[16]

The vast second problem concerns the formation and meaning of the part of the Iranian *Book of Kings* which comes before the strangely selective treatment of the Achaemenid reigns, limited to those of the two "Dārās"; that is, the Great Darius and the last one; the loser of Marathon and the hapless adversary of Alexander, outfitted with lineages and events wholly at variance with what is known from other sources.

These beginnings essentially consist of three groups of kings:[17] (1) the three whom Arthur Christensen has called the "first kings"[18] because, although they are presented successively in a historical order, each of them could have been, and before the fixing of this canon undoubtedly was, a "first king": a universal and civilizing one; (2) a series of kings, forming a dynasty, whose kinship ties are not always certain: the kavis, or, as they are called in the West from the Middle Iranian plural form of their name, the "Kayanids"; (3) more or less clearly linked with the kavis, a succession of kings (including one queen) who are particularly important in that it is under one of them that tradition places the teaching and early successes of Zoroaster.

As with all accounts that the learned men of any people have made of their early centuries, the difficulty lies in determining at what point true history begins, after all the fanciful tales of first beginnings. It is always here that a kind of schism inevitably sets specialist against comparativist, the first more inclined to credit the

[16] Hildegard Lewy, "The Babylonian Background of the Kay Kaus Legend," *Archiv Orientální* 17 (1949): 28–109, arbitrarily reducing the entire legend of this king to a few features (some secondary, others distorted), has tried to derive it from "events" of the reign of the Babylonian king Nabu-nā-īd (Nabonidus), and has not hesitated to involve Cambyses in the matter.

[17] Stig Wikander, "Sur le fonds commun indo-iranien des épopées de la Perse et de l'Inde," *La Nouvelle Clio* 2 ([1949–]1950): 310–329.

[18] *Les types du premier homme et du premier roi dans l'histoire légendaire des Iraniens* (*Archives Orientales*, publ. by J.-A. Lundell, XIV, I [1917]; II [1934]).

texts, seeing in the most legendary scenes real events that simply have been embellished, and the second quick to find in the same scenes themes so well attested elsewhere that they can dispense with the events. For these debates Iran provides a wealth of subject matter.

Both sides seem to be agreed in abandoning to legend, and even to mythology, the three "first kings" Haošyaŋha, Taxma Urupi, and Yima Xšaēta: does not the third carry the name of an assuredly Indo-Iranian legendary figure? It is on the second and third series of kings that disagreement arises.

The great majority of Iranianists support the authenticity of the Kayanids. From Arthur Christensen to Mary Boyce, the most important writers see in this dynasty, at least on the whole, a piece of history on a level with the Achaemenids, the Arsacids, and the Sassanians. Christensen's opinion was unqualified. He had no love for the "comparative mythology" he had known in his youth, and as early as 1917, in the preface to his book on the first kings, he summarily condemned a great work, one no doubt antiquated but not wholly outdated, in which many conclusions remain today as important as Christensen's own—and this is no small praise.

> James Darmesteter [he wrote[19]] has added much new material to the study of Iranian legends, but he has treated these matters primarily from the point of view of comparative mythology, a kind of discipline that, owing to a method devoid of any critical judgment, has been entirely discredited.

In 1931 in his book *Les Kayanides,*[20] published before the second part of his *Types du premier homme,* he stated a principle that can be far reaching, and, naturally, accused his potential detractors of wishing to be right "at all costs":

> Faced with accounts that claim to be historical, and whose general nature does not necessarily preclude a historical reality, the sound method is, in my view, not to look for

[19] *Les types du premier homme* I: 3.

[20] *Les Kayanides* (Copenhagen, 1931), p. 30.

myths in them at all costs, but to consider these accounts as having at least a basis in truth.

Twenty-three years later, the brilliant Mary Boyce herself bravely undertook to discover how, through the channel of what literary genres, a history of such high caliber could have been preserved:[21]

> That some secular records, presumably oral, existed in Vištāspa's own days [i.e., in the time of the patron of Zoroaster] is to be assumed from the fact that we still possess an account, altered and doubtless dignified by the passage of time, of the battles, raids and blood-feuds of his ancestors to the sixth generation. Memories of such exploits are most likely to have been kept alive if enshrined soon after the event in some formal manner; and the nature of the account which has come down to us suggests strongly that its origin is to be traced, not to genealogical tables and antiquarian catalogues (although such doubtless existed at the time), but to a court-poetry of celebration and entertainment, characteristic of a heroic age.

On an objective discussion of these matters, beyond personal impressions and short of preformed convictions, we have only a single handle, but a substantial one: one of the two Kayanids about whom Iranian tradition knows the most is this Kavi Usa(δa)n whose name closely recalls the Indic Kāvya Uśanas. Depending on whether correspondences beyond the agreement of names in the types of these characters and in their actions can or cannot be recognized and specified, the thesis of Christensen and Boyce will lose or gain ground. In the first case, the interpretation

[21] P. 46 of "Some Remarks on the Transmission of the Kayanian Heroic Cycle," *Serta Cantabrigiensia* (1954), pp. 45–52. On the Indian side, I quote for the record a sentence of Jarl Charpentier in one of his most debatable essays, "Indra, ein Versuch der Aufklärung," *Le Monde Oriental* 25 (1931): 24: "There are also certain figures surrounding Indra—such as Kutsa (for whom the extant Old Iranian tradition provides no counterpart) or Kavi Uśanas (Uśanas Kāvya) (who corresponds to the Avestan Kava Usa)—who seem to me quite definitely to contain traces of an erstwhile human existence" [trans. from German].

of the rule of Kavi Usa(δa)n as historicized myth will be plausible, and the more probable as the thematic correspondences that are uncovered become more numerous and precise. In the second case, one will be free to play the little game of history and to imagine that the story of this kavi's reign reports, just as we read it, a series of real happenings, simply "altered and doubtless dignified by the passage of time," but luckily saved, not by conscientious genealogists, but by punctilious court poets. The Indic Kāvya Uśanas is thus found to be the key to the most important problem of the historiography of pre-Zoroastrian Iran, as well as to the problem of "comparative Indo-Iranian epic" which is raised by his very name.

The first sketch of this study, begun in 1958, was made public at eight lectures at the Collège de France, from 4 November 1965 to 6 January 1966. The general outline was presented in three seminars at the Center for Indo-European Studies of the University of California at Los Angeles in January 1971.

I

1887–1939

1. KĀVYA UŚANAS AND KAVI USA(ΔA)N (KAY ŪS, KAŪS)

In 1887, when Friedrich von Spiegel was about to draw up his summary and prospectus on Indo-Iranian epic, the comparative dossier of Kāvya Uśanas and Kavi Usan was limited to a few items, as only the oldest texts were willingly considered.

In the *ṚgVeda* a mythical character, who is neither a god nor a hero but a wise and powerful sort of holy man, is called by the Vedic poets by the name Uśana-, which seems to be derived from the root *vaś-* ("wish," as in Greek ἑκών). Before being normalized with -s in the epic language, the Vedic declension presents some anomalies: the nominative, accusative, and dative are in the *Ṛg-Veda* those of an -ā- stem; the locative and, in one of the variants of the single attestation in the *Atharva Veda*, the accusative are those of an -a- stem.[1] There is also uncertainty over the meaning of

[1] Wackernagel-Debrunner, *Altindische Grammatik* III (Göttingen, 1930): 285 [trans. from German]:

"The inflection of *uśánā-* is irregular (originally abstract fem. in *ā-*, whence instr. sg. adv. Ved. *uśánā*, 'eagerly, hastily' [J. Schmidt, *KZ* 26, 402 n.]?, or originally *n*-stem **uśanan-*, whence haplologically dat. **uśan[an]e*?), name of a prehistoric sage: Ved. nom. sg. *uśánā*, acc. sg. *-ām* *RV* 10.40.7b (and *AV* 4.29.6b, where Paipp. has *uśánam*), dat. sg. *-e* (as from *ā*-stems) *RV* 6.20.11b, loc. sg. *-e* (as from *a*-stems) *RV* 1.51.11a. *JB* 1.130 and Class. Skt. stem *uśanas-* with nom. sg. *uśanā*, as Pāṇini also requires (but Epic *uśanāḥ*); see also §150 a A.; for the voc. sg.

an instrumental *uśánā*, which some connect with the proper name (thus meaning "with Uśanas"), and others interpret as an adverb ("willingly, with eagerness"), and which, depending on the alternative one chooses, adds to the inventory or excludes from consideration a large number of passages.

Moreover, this name is frequently accompanied by the epithet *kā́vya*, preceding or following, which can mean either "son of kaví" or "of the nature or number of the kavís," and he is himself once called kaví. This figure does not play a large part in the hymns, and most of the texts where he does appear remain obscure, alluding to poorly known mythical activities. At least he is taken as a model, a standard (*uśáneva*, "like Uśanas") of knowledge, spoken (*ṚgVeda* 4.16.2, 9.97.7) or applied (9.87.3). Along the same lines, he gives good advice: when embarking on a difficult expedition, Indra and the human hero who accompanies him come to take counsel with Uśanas, and when they arrive he asks them—this is one of the clearest texts (10.22.6)—:

> Why have you two come to our house from afar,
> from heaven and earth, to a mortal?[2]

The hymn does not give the visitors' answer, but other texts show that Indra leaves his host's home in very fine fettle (*mándiṣṭha*, 1.51.11), gorged with intoxicating (*mandína*, 1.121.12) soma and endowed with "a power that Uśanas made for him with might" (*tákṣad yát ta uśánā sáhasā sáhaḥ*, 1.51.10) or, more concretely, "with the weapon that kills Vṛtrá" and determines the outcome of battle (*vṛtrahánaṃ pā́ryam tatakṣa vájram*, 1.121.12). Two other texts seem to attribute to Uśanas an important role in the establishment of the first sacrifice: he installed Fire as *hótar*, the chanting priest (8.23.17), and he "gathered the cows" (1.83.5).

Kāś. (ad Pāṇ. 7.1.94) gives the choice of *uśanaḥ* (from stem *uśanas-*) or *uśanan* (from nom. sg. *uśanā* [Benfey, *Gött. Abh.* 17, 85] or *uśana* (after the *a*-stems)."

[2] *kádarthā na ā́ gṛhám*
ā́ jagmathuḥ parākā́d
diváś ca gmáś ca mártyam

In the post-Gāthic *Avesta*, a figure named Kavi- Usan- (nominative, Kava Usa) appears twice. The Yašt of the god of aggressive victory Vərəϑragna (*Yašt* 14, 39–40) says that the bird Vārəngan, the falcon, one of this god's incarnations, possesses a miraculous strength, the same as that held by Kavi Usan and also by Θraētaona, slayer of the dragon Dahāka. In the Yašt of the Patroness of Waters, Arədvī Sūrā (*Yašt* 5, 45–47), Kavi Usan appears in the long list of persons who have sacrificed to the goddess in order to gain specific ends, his prayer and its outcome being thus: "May I attain highest sovereignty over all countries, over *daēvas* and men, over male and female sorcerers, over the kavi and *karapan* potentates." Unfortunately this request, though it ranks him among sovereign rulers, is not his alone: it matches in the same Yašt those of two of his mythic predecessors, Haošyaŋha Paraδāta (22) and Yima (26), and one of his successors, Haosravah (50).

In addition, two other Yašts (those of Fravaši [13, 132] and Earth [19, 71]) present a Kavi Usaδan, who is surely the same, as the third in the list of eight figures called kavi—the epic Kayanids—but give no information about him.

Of course it was well known over a hundred years ago that the Indic epic on one hand and the Pahlavi texts and the epics of Islamic Iran on the other have more to say about these two nearly homonymous characters. But the prestige of the *Ṛg Veda* and the *Avesta*, together with the postulate—explicit or implicit—which made, and often still makes, the most ancient writings the best evidence for a tradition, did not encourage such a descent through the centuries down to the *Mahābhārata* and Firdausi. Moreover, at first sight, the epic narratives of India and Iran seemed to have nothing in common, which confirmed, it was thought, that they were simply divergent proliferations starting from the meager data of the Vedic hymns and the Zoroastrian Yašts.

Under these circumstances, the consensus among philologists was that the agreement of the two names Kāvya- (kavi-) Uśana(s)- and Kavi- Usan- (Usaδan-), despite their slight dissimilarity, did indeed indicate that the Indo-Iranians knew a legendary figure who bore a name similar to these, but that nothing could be determined about this figure by comparison of the texts where these names are found. In these extremely early times, either he had had a very vague personality that the Indians and Iranians had later fleshed out in quite independent ways, or more precise legends had existed that had been forgotten on both sides, or at least on one side, and replaced by new material.

2. FRIEDRICH VON SPIEGEL (1871, 1877)

In 1887, Spiegel made a remark that could have gotten the study under way. In fact, the practitioners of "comparative mythology," less convinced than the philologists that all comparison must be by way of the *ṚgVeda* and the *Avesta*, had long since considered the epic traditions. Following up a suggestion of Adalbert Kuhn, Spiegel himself had written as early as 1871:[3]

> The very name of the Vedic Kāvya Uśanas so closely resembles that of the Kava Uśan of the Iranians that one cannot help but suppose a relationship between the two figures. We believe we have also found this connection in an ascension to heaven (*Himmelsfahrt*) in which the Iranian Usan falls down, as does in India, not Kāvya Uśanas himself to be sure, but his son-in-law, who on account of his pride is thrown from heaven back down to earth. Moreover this myth is in origin already Indo-European; the Greek myth of Daedalus and the German one of Wieland the Smith vividly recall it, the more so as the Iranian Kava Usan also appears as an artisan, under whose orders the demons are forced to work.

As with many of the collocations of the Kuhnian school, this one was inconclusive: aside from the fact that it is not true that

[3] *Eranische Alterthumskunde I (Geographie, Ethnographie und älteste Geschichte)* (Leipzig, 1871): 441.

Kavi Usan, in the epic, is an "artisan" (Louis XIV was no artisan when he ordered the building of Versailles), one cannot in this manner substitute the son-in-law for the father-in-law in a comparison. Moreover, the case of Yayāti, son-in-law of Kāvya Uśanas in the epic, is quite different from that of Kay Ūs or Kay Kaūs—Pahlavi and Persian forms of Kavi Usan: the latter tries, out of pride, to get to heaven by a plan of aggression and conquest, and finds himself thrown down before getting there; the former, after having been welcomed by the gods after his death and having remained among them for centuries in reward for an extremely virtuous life, is unable one day to contain a prideful thought, which, canceling his merits, plummets him back down to earth.

Spiegel himself undoubtedly recognized the weakness of this comparison, for in 1887, in his second book, *Die arische Periode und ihre Zustände,* while retaining the *Himmelsfahrt* as a secondary argument, he emphasized another more important correspondence, equally post-Vedic and post-Avestan.[4]

After stating that, "as usual," neither the *ṚgVeda* nor the *Avesta* gives enough substance to the two figures to permit a useful comparison, he notes that on one hand, in the *Mahābhārata* as in the *Rāmāyaṇa,* Kāvya Uśanas is the "tutor of the Asuras"—that is, the demons who are the gods' rivals—and because of his magical knowledge is their invaluable ally in the struggle that they undertake against the gods. On the other hand, in the *Shāh Nāmeh,* Kay Kaūs not only subjugates the demons to his power as is told already in *Yašt* 5, but goes on to turn them into his workers for spectacular construction projects, and also allows himself to be beguiled by them, and on their advice, at the head of their army, sets himself at war against God for the conquest of heaven. Thus the two characters, both men, or rather supermen, appear either on the side or at the head of the demons, and together with them, as their collaborator or at their instigation, as adversaries of God or the gods.

[4] Pp. 281–287.

Here in fact is a noteworthy and unassailable accordance, one that reaches to the heart of characters as well as actions: despite the differences of religion, in the polytheism of the *Mahābhārata* as in Zoroastrian monotheism prolonged by that of Islam, this kavi or kāvya is involved on the side of the demons in one episode in their long conflict with the celestial beings. A closer examination of the texts, even as early as this, would have made it possible to give more precision and detail to this correspondence, and to unravel others from it which would match and reinforce it. But the decisive step had been taken.

3. 1887–1939

No doubt it was already too late in the century for a younger scholar to dare to explore the way thus opened. At the level of the gods and their exploits, "comparative mythology" was rapidly being discredited; was there any use in extending its mirages to heroes and their legends? Spiegel's comment did not raise a ripple; more precisely, it was forgotten. The half century from 1887 to 1938 saw the appearance of great philologists, several of whom were men of genius; the study of the *Avesta* and Middle Iranian texts and of Vedic literature, if not the epic, made steady progress, but the typological comparison of Kavi Usan and Kāvya Uśanas, neglected and rejected, gained nothing from it.

The situation was even more serious. Disengaged from the disreputable and moribund "comparative mythology," linguistics in those days became lean and mean. Strict grammarians taught that because it was not precise the agreement of the two names was of no interest: Was it not an illusion, an approximation, like so many other equations about which the Max Müller school had dreamed; like *Kéntauros-Gandharvá* especially, which phonetic laws, they said, would no longer allow to be retained (even though the Greek Centaur was a man with the crupper of a horse and the epic Gandharva a horse with the bust of a man)? It is true that the

Indic forms Uśanas, Uśanā match in Avestan neither Usan nor Usaδan. Furthermore, although the title kavi in Iran consistently occurs with Usan or Usaδan (even to the point of having produced by reduplication the epic onomastic monstrosity Kay Kaūs), kāvya, which is moreover only a derivative of kavi, does not necessarily accompany Uśanas either in the hymns or in the epic. This criticism was pushed to the extreme by a linguist to whom Avestan studies owe a large part of their rapid progress, Christian Bartholomae: in 1905, in his admirable *Altiranisches Wörterbuch*, s.v. *Usan*, he interpreted this word as an adjective derived from an unattested **usa*, which would correspond exactly to Sanskrit *utsa*, "spring," and likewise Usaδan as an adjective derived from a compound **u(t)sa-dā-*, comparable with Sanskrit *utsa-dhí*: these two variants would mean equally "rich in springs." He concluded disdainfully, alluding perhaps to Spiegel: "I have not succeeded in discovering the supposed connections with the Indic Uśanas kāvya. If my etymology is correct, the resemblance of the names evaporates in turn."

Bartholomae has not been followed, but whether they be sensitive or indifferent to the similarity of the names, Indianists and Iranianists have been in accord in making no further attempt to compare the figures. Ten years after *Die arische Periode*, in 1897, in the second volume of the *Vedische Studien* (where, with Karl F. Geldner and against Abel Bergaigne and Hermann Oldenberg, he established successfully by many examples that it is impossible to deprive Vedic exegesis of the aid of later literature, and the *Mahābhārata* in particular), Richard Pischel studied Kāvya Uśanas at length in connection with the myth of Kutsa.[5] Composing a new summary of the Vedic and post-Vedic facts concerning him, he analyzed more precisely than Spiegel had done the episode of Kāvya Uśanas in the first book of the *Mahābhārata*. Not once does he mention the Iranian Kavi Usaδan, Kay Ūs, Kay Kaūs, nor does he cite Spiegel. He even allows what progress the latter had made to be lost, and casts an important feature back into the indeter-

[5] *Vedische Studien* II (Stuttgart, 1897): 166–170.

minacy from which it had been extracted, suggesting that, in contrast to the *Ṛg Veda*, the *Brāhmaṇas* and the *Mahābhārata* may have innovated by making Kāvya Uśanas the chaplain of the demons. At least Pischel was only an Indianist. The case of his colleague Geldner, to whom Avestan studies no less than Vedic are indebted, is more odd. In his annotated translation of the *Ṛg Veda*, he encounters Kāvya Uśanas some fifteen times: nowhere does he feel the need to recall the nearly homonymous Kavi Usan, to whose explication via the *Bundahišn*, the *Dēnkart*, and Firdausi he should have been led by a natural extension of the method of the *Vedische Studien*. It is an extreme example of the tendency toward "specialization of studies," Jean Filliozat has said[6] in connection with precisely the case under discussion, that Geldner, "at once Iranianist and Vedic scholar, practiced his two specialties as virtually divorced from one another, even though they have to do in large measure with contiguous ideas and expressions, appearing among peoples of common origin and in constant communication." Another first-rate Iranianist, Arthur Christensen, could write in 1931 a most valuable essay on the Kayanids, gather in detail what Zoroastrian and Islamic Iran of all periods had said about Kavi Usan, and still avoid casting a glance at India—he mentions Kāvya Uśanas only in a footnote to discard him, not even imagining that there might be an Indo-Iranian problem here, and admitting at the most the theoretical possibility of a borrowing by India from Iran:[7]

> Has the Uśanas Kāvya of the Vedas anything to do with Kavi Usaδan (Usan)? Could allusions to this powerful kavi have been insinuated into the *Ṛg Veda?* This is for Vedicists to decide. It would not be surprising that the renown of the kavis could have penetrated into the Indus Valley, communications with the Aryans of India being easier than those that existed between the tribes of eastern and western Iran, who were separated by great deserts.

[6] *Annuaire du Collège de France*, 1954, pp. 241–242.
[7] *Les Kayanides*, p. 28, n. 2.

4. HERMAN LOMMEL (1939)

It remained for one of the most open and independent minds of our time, Herman Lommel, another Indianist and Iranian specialist, to put an end to this segregation of fields that in the guise of prudence and modesty made impossible the maturation and even the formulation of real problems. In 1939, he picked up the study where Spiegel had left it and by the same method, with more rigor and insight, isolated a second accordance. First, however, publishing his treatment in a testimonial volume dedicated to one of the main disciples of Ferdinand de Saussure,[8] he resolved like a linguist the minor but real difficulty posed by the imperfect agreement of the names, Indic Uśanas (-nā) versus Iranian Usan (Usaδan).

The simplest form of the Indic name, he said, was *Uśan, corresponding exactly to the Avestan short form; the forms with -as-, -ā-, and -a-, mingled in a motley declension by the ṚgVedic poets, are various enlargements of it, as is also the Avestan long form Usaδan. This *Uśan is not directly attested but is assured by the adjective derived from it. The liturgical texts in fact have the adjective *auśana*, a regular formation with maximum lengthening (*vṛddhi*) of the vowel in the first syllable (cf. *brahman* ~ *brāhmaṇa*), which the Indian grammarians viewed as the adjective corresponding to the name of Kāvya Uśanas. The grammarians were correct, because in the sūtras, the melody (*sāman*) of a ṚgVedic hymn (to Agni, 8.84.1–3) purported to be the work of Uśanā Kāvyaḥ is called *auśanam sāma*. This proof is, however, less complete than Lommel thought, because an adjective auśana can correspond to a noun in -na just as well as to one in -n (cf. *raudra*, "pertaining to Rudra," *bauddha*, "follower of Buddha," etc.), and because part of the composite declension of Uśanas is indeed built on a stem *Uśana-. It is nevertheless clear that the form with -s-, the furthest removed from the Avestan form, provides no further objection as it is in any case an enlargement.

[8] "Kāvya Uçan," *Mélanges de linguistique offerts à Charles Bally* (Geneva, 1939), pp. 209–214; followed by a second essay, "Der Welt-Ei-Mythos im Rig Veda," pp. 214–220.

As for the authenticity of the connection of the two parts of the name, Kāvya (sometimes kavi) and Uśanas, Lommel made some useful comments: (1) If it happens that Uśanas is named without Kāvya, there are other cases where he is called Kāvya without Uśanas; therefore it seems that the name was indeed a composite one, but that the analysis of its elements remained transparent, so that the *ṛṣis* freely used sometimes the full form, sometimes one or the other element indifferently. (2) The case of Kāvya (kavi) Uśanas is unique; already Abel Bergaigne had noted that there is no other kavi in the *ṚgVeda* with whose name this title is so closely linked. (3) Even in Iran, the connection of kavi with Usan must have been particularly close, because although kavi is the common title of the eight kings of the Kayanid dynasty, this one is the only one in whose name this title has been welded to the proper name (Kay Ūs, Kaūs), to the point where a new Kay (< kavi, or even <kāvya?) has been preposed, to replace what was no longer perceived: Kay Kaūs.

Having thus resolved or attenuated the formal difficulties, Lommel takes up again the comparison of the legendary figures by referring to Spiegel. He does so very tactfully, emphasizing first of all, better than his predecessor, that whatever its explanation, the semantic difference observable between the Vedic kavi, a kind of holy man, and the Avestan kavi, a kind of temporal chieftain, could not fail to lead in two different directions the character, activity, and exploits of a presumed Indo-Iranian *Kavi *Uśan. This fine scholar writes as follows:[9]

> Thus if there existed an Indo-Iranian legendary figure whose name and nature had become closely associated with the word and concept of kavi-, then for that reason the saga figure itself had to undergo strongly divergent developments among the two peoples, appearing here as a Brahman, there as a king.
>
> In the *Mahābhārata* (Calc. I 3185ff., Bomb. 76, Poona 1.71 [van Buitenen pp. 175ff.]), in the struggle between the gods and the Asuras, Kāvya Uśanas is the priestly helper of

[9] Art. cit. in footnote 8, pp. 211–214.

the demons—as is attested already in Vedic times (see Geldner, *Vedische Studien* II:167)—as the priest-god Bṛhaspati is the *purohita* of the gods. But Uśanas is superior to Bṛhaspati in that he possesses the magical knowledge of how to reawaken the dead. Because he continually calls back to life all the Asuras who fall in the war against the gods, all the efforts of the gods to defeat the demons are doomed to failure until they succeed in tricking the secret magic out of him.

The Iranian King Kay Kaūs considers himself mightier than any king before him, and in his arrogance undertakes the dangerous venture of conquering the Māzandarān, the land of the *dīvs* (demons). Despite disastrous failures he succeeds, mainly through the heroic deeds of Rustam, and thus Kay Kaūs becomes master of the demons as well. They erect marvelous magic castles for him in the Elburz Mountains, where eternal spring and youth reign and aged men become young. But the demons seduce him into the foolish plan, now that he has lorded it over the whole world, over men and demons, of attempting to conquer heaven too. He has himself carried up by eagles, but falls pitifully to the ground. In spite of his serious transgression, because he repents the favor of heaven is restored to him and he continues to rule. Arbitrariness, caprice, and thoughtlessness are the hallmarks of his reign, yet the might of the Iranian throne is greater than ever under him, and it is while he is king that the most famous exploits of Rustam take place, including his tragic battle with his son Sōhrab. In this connection, it is said that Kay Kaūs possesses a balm that could heal the mortal wounds of Sōhrab. And this is the most despicable feature in the whole image of Kay Kaūs, that he refuses to provide this marvelous remedy, because Rustam and Sōhrab together, if both were alive, would be too powerful for him.

Even with as many unpleasant things as Firdausi has to report about Kay Kaūs, one does not have the impression that it is his intention to defame him or depict him as an evil man; moreover, the fact that this magic balm, which would have been most useful to him in his risky and often unsuccessful campaigns, is mentioned nowhere else leads one to conclude that this feature was not invented by Firdausi, but was traditional. How old a trait this is and whether it is related to the magical resuscitative power of Kāvya Uśanas admittedly cannot be said with certainty. But rather than summarily disavowing all connections, one should at least consider this motif.

Then, in an extension of what Spiegel had already discovered, Lommel writes:

> But in the older tradition, of which Christensen in the aforementioned work [*Les Kayanides*] offers us such an excellent survey, appears yet another support for a comparison of this kind, one that of course must be attempted only as an experiment within the already described perspective of a considerable evolutionary development of the legendary material. In the *Shāh Nāmeh*, Kay Kaūs, senseless as his war against the Māzandarān may be, is on this occasion at least a fighter on the right side and conqueror of the worst demons. In the earlier tradition (Christensen, 73–74, 108–109) he does not fight against the demons but is their ruler, and while in Firdausi his rising to heaven on the throne carried by eagles is more an absurd and foolish adventure than a sacrilege, in the Pahlavi texts his assault on heaven at the head of his demonic forces, notwithstanding its complete hopelessness against the One God, seems more serious. This could after all correspond to the war, led by Kāvya Uśanas, of the Asuras against the gods. The Middle Iranian tradition reports still more evil misdeeds of Kay Kaūs (Christensen, p 75f.), and it seems that Firdausi, because this king had belonged to the glorious national tradition, has brightened his character somewhat and softened his crimes into foibles.
>
> Unfortunately, neither the *Avesta* nor Sanskrit tradition offers more precise possibilities for comparison. . . . Thus the data are insufficient to carry out a convincing collation of the legends. Yet I believe that here, as so often, the early period of Indo-Iranian philology shows more insight than later scholarship, so often inhibited by criticism and skepticism. For there

is no fact that compels or entitles us to separate the related names; rather I think I have adduced some viewpoints from which, great divergences notwithstanding, a kinship of the legends seems probable.

Here too we should not lose sight of the scholarly task before us, namely the recognition of the elements common to India and Iran.

By repeating such rhetorical warnings, despite his own obvious inclination, did Lommel intend to disarm his critics? In any case, this "new fact" has not registered on Indianists or Iranianists. With the help of the disturbances of World War II, it remained unknown. But it is striking nonetheless. The fact that two homonymous heroes are endowed with the same power against death—how can this be ascribed to chance?

So much for the history of the problem. It is short, as we see, and hinges on two dates, 1887 and 1939. Let us now return to the study systematically, in order to spell out and evaluate those accordances already identified and, if possible, to discover others.

II

THE STORY OF KĀVYA UŚANAS

1. KĀVYA UŚANAS IN THE GENEALOGY OF THE PĀṆḌAVAS

The tale of Kāvya Uśanas in the first book of the *Mahābhārata*[1] is set into the lengthy introduction of the ancestors of the two groups of first cousins who confront each other throughout the greater part of the epic—not because they have even the least drop of this character's blood in their veins, but because, when they find themselves the holders of, or pretenders to, the throne in the "central fifth" of the world, it is as a direct result of one of his intercessions. And we should not forget that this intervention is, moreover, quite close to the beginnings, taking place in the time and context of one of the legendary princes who are the first members of the lunar dynasty. Dakṣa, functioning here as creator, took as his son-in-law, among others, Kaśyapa, resulting first in the birth of the three pairs of Ādityas, the sovereign gods, then two other twins, the god Indra and Vivasvat, the latter an ill-defined being on the borderline between human and divine. Vivasvat had two

[1] Book I, Calcutta 75–85 (*ślokas* 3183–3534); Poona 71–80; J. A. B. van Buitenen (trans.), *The Mahābhārata* I (Chicago, 1973): 175–194. The term "tale" is used here without prejudice to the literary form. Van Buitenen, presenting the text of the *Mahābhārata*, inclines to the layout of a theatrical composition—numerous dialogues, easy division into acts and scenes, etc.

equally famous sons, Yama and Manu, the first of whom became king of the abode of the dead. The second, the ancestor and eponym of mankind, was through his daughter Iḷā (an ancient Vedic goddess of libation) the originator of the lunar dynasty: his grandson Purūravas, well known for his relationship with the Apsaras Urvaśī and his entanglements with Gandharvas and brahmins alike, begat six sons, among whom was Āyu, the personification of the life force. Āyu had four sons, including Nahuṣa, who is in this context an entirely upright king. Finally, Nahuṣa had six sons, the second of whom, Yayāti, for better or worse, encounters Kāvya Uśanas and marries his daughter. One of Yayāti's sons (but not by this woman), Pūru, will be the ancestor of the Pauravas, the heroes of the epic, and when Pūru, even though he is the last born, receives the kingship instead of his four brothers, it is by a sort of permission granted to his father by Kāvya Uśanas. Thus the poets had good reason to linger, at this particular point in the genealogy, on this character who does not belong to the race whose deeds, faults, and misfortunes they record. His tale is not a parenthesis in the story; it is rather, one might say, a turning point. It is, moreover, very tightly constructed: none of the successive events, however small, in which Kāvya Uśanas is involved and which result in Pūru's accession to the kingship could be omitted. They are the continuous links of a long and truly causal chain; as Kāvya Uśanas's daughter herself puts it at one critical point, "we are witnessing fate at work."

His powers and pretentions notwithstanding, Kāvya Uśanas is no more than a tool of this fate, the same as the lesser lords whom he champions or intimidates. If fate has elected to make use of him, it is because his nature is suited either to move or to point events in the desired direction. For destiny—and this is what creates the pathos of the dramas which it inspires—rarely forces men; it is satisfied with helping them to develop the natural strengths and weaknesses that define them. The poets who were interpreters and, after all, authors of destiny thus had an interest, on the one hand, in respecting scrupulously, and on the other, in expounding clearly and at length what tradition provided them about this character. We have in our turn only to follow their narration, noting as we go the characteristics unfolded there. Thus the reader will see that from the standpoint of Kāvya Uśanas the novel comprises three episodes. In the first and the third it presents—and each time this is the mainspring for the action—his two unique capabilities: in the first episode the formula for resuscitating the dead, and in the third the power of transforming old age into youth and vice versa. In the intervening episode he defines, declares, and realizes his ambitions regarding both demons and royalty. The complex and coherent figure drawn from these observations will prove amenable to overall comparison with the Iranian data.

2. KĀVYA UŚANAS, CHAPLAIN OF THE DEMONS, AND THE SECRET OF RESURRECTION

As it did already in Vedic prose literature, the opposition of the gods and the demons, of *devas* (or *suras*) and *asuras* (or *dānavas*), takes the form in the epic of a war between two peoples, each with an army, its capital, and its king. What we see is not individual deeds, duels between Indra and one or another great demon; it is a clash of two orderly societies. The poet does not take sides; he does not attribute all the wrongdoing to the demons, and he does not even give the impression that a demonic victory would have particularly changed the order, morality, and customs that we live by and to which, on the whole, they too conform. The control or the sovereignty (the *aiśvarya*) would simply have been in other hands.

Each of the two sides has its *purohita*, its officiating priest, who is at the same time its religious counselor and even, by virtue of the "knowledge" in which he specializes, its helper in military activity. The purohita whom the gods have chosen (*vavrire*) is himself a god, Bṛhaspati, the mythic projection of the *brahman*, while the demons have retained the services of a descendant of Bhṛgu, Kāvya Uśanas. Despite the disparity of their natures, the god Bṛhaspati and the superman Kāvya Uśanas find themselves equals both in their function and in their competition (*nityam anyonyaspherdinau bhṛśam*), and they both carry the title of *brāhmaṇa*. We may suppose that this is a distortion of a tradition that, before the establishment of the strict system of *varṇas*, must have allowed (as was still the case in the Vedic hymns) for several types of holy man: the kaví, more a magician, was not equivalent to the sacrificing priests. The *Mahābhārata*'s account has been unable to eliminate an essential trace of this ancient state of affairs: in at least one regard, a truly magical one, the superiority is not on the side of the chaplain-god, but on that of the sorcerer Kāvya (van Buitenen, p. 176):

> The gods killed off the Dānavas who had gathered for battle, but Uśanas drew on the power of his knowledge and returned them to life. They stood up again and warred on the gods. The Asuras in turn cut down the gods in the thick of the battle, but the wise Bṛhaspati could not revive them; for he did not have that knowledge that the mighty Uśanas possessed, the knowledge of revivification, and so the gods became utterly desperate.
>
> The gods, affrighted of Uśanas Kāvya, went to Kaca,[2] the eldest son of Bṛhaspati, and spoke to him.

They beg him to go, invoking the solidarity of this supranational guild which includes holy men on all sides, and present himself to Kāvya as an apprentice, to get from him as quickly as possible (*āhara kṣipram*) the knowledge that resides in him. "You can find the brahmin at Vṛṣaparvan's [the king of the demons]; there he grants his protection to the Dānavas but refuses it to all others." Kaca should gain the master's favor, and also, above all, by his gentility and good manners (moral rather than physical attributes), he should secure the cooperation of Devayānī, Kāvya's

[2] Pronounced "KA-cha."

much-beloved daughter. If he pleases her, they say, he cannot fail to obtain the knowledge without which the gods will perish.[3] Kaca consents and goes to Kāvya, to the court of the enemy king. He presents himself as what he is; what has he to fear? The priestly assistants of belligerents are rivals to be sure, but they themselves are not at war; class or professional solidarity is stronger than the fleeting circumstances or contractual obligations that oppose them. Nonetheless, he does not tell Kāvya the ultimate purpose of his enterprise:

> "Sir, accept me, the grandson of Angiras and son of Bṛhaspati himself, who am named Kaca, as your own student. I shall do my most chaste studies with you as my teacher. Approve me, brahmin, for a thousand years."

Without asking for further explanation, the master replies:

> "Be warmly welcome, Kaca. I shall accept your word. I shall honor you who deserve honor, and Bṛhaspati too shall thus be honored."

The spiritual idyll begun so well unfolds. Father and daughter, especially the daughter, are won over by this splendid young man. Every day he gives Devayānī her share of singing, dancing, and music, brings her flowers and fruit, and makes himself her knight in waiting. Nor is she in arrears: she too delights him with her songs and attentions. Five hundred years go by in this way, half of an exceptionally pleasant novitiate. Never is there any mention of the precious secret that it is Kaca's mission to acquire, surprise being of the essence. But around this charming trio others are watching. The demons take a dim view of the son of the gods' priest lingering thus with their own chaplain, and suspect that their privilege of resuscitation is in danger. Then one day (p. 177),

> They found him herding cows in the wilderness and alone. Secretly, without compunction, they killed him out of hatred for Bṛhaspati, and also to safeguard the magic knowledge.

[3] Van Buitenen, *Mahābhārata* I: 176.

> And after killing him they cut him into pieces the size of sesamum seeds and fed him to the jackals.
>
> The cattle later returned to their habitation, without their cowherd. When Devayānī saw that the cows had come back from the woods without Kaca, she spoke up at once. . . . "The *agnihotra* has not been offered yet," she said, "and the sun has set, my lord. The cows have come back without their herdsman. Kaca is nowhere to be found, father. Surely Kaca must have been killed, father, or have died! Without him I cannot live, I tell you the truth!"

Kāvya is not disturbed:

> "If he is dead, I shall call him and say, 'Come back!' And I will revive him."
>
> He employed his reviving knowledge and called Kaca. And by this magic Kaca reappeared happily as soon as he was called, piercing the sides of the wolves and springing out.[4]

The demons refuse to consider themselves beaten. Some recensions of the *Mahābhārata* credit them with up to three killings, in keeping with a well-known pattern of this type of tale. But the second, echoing the first, does not appear in several others: one day when Devayānī has sent Kaca to the woods to get her some flowers, the demons kill him, cut him to pieces and throw the pieces into the sea, and it is from deep in the waters that Kāvya, at his daughter's entreaty, must once again recall and restore his student. In any case, be it second or third, the last attempt does credit to the demons' cleverness. The imprudent girl has again asked the lad to bring her a bouquet. And so he goes out, and then,

> They killed him a second time, burned him, ground the ashes to dust, and then the Asuras fed him to the brahmin in his wine. And once more Devayānī said to her father: "Kaca went out on an errand to pluck flowers; father, he is nowhere to be seen!"

[4] *āhūtaḥ prādhur abhavat kaco 'riṣṭo 'tha vidyayā*
bhittvā bhittvā śarīrāṇi vṛkānāṃ sa viniṣpatat

This time, the father hesitates to use his knowledge—he is ready to accept the inescapable:

> "He is Bṛhaspati's son, daughter. If Kaca went out on the journey of the dead and has been killed, even though he owed his life to my magic, what am I to do?
>
> Do not sorrow like this or weep, Devayānī—
> Your likes shall not grieve over mortal man.
> All the gods and the world entire
> Must bow to the change that impends."

Fine advice for a daughter in love! She protests:

> "His grandfather is the ancient Angiras,
> His father ascetic Bṛhaspati—
> Son and grandson of a seer,
> Should I not mourn over him and weep?
>
> My fellow-student is he, an ascetic,
> Always alert and skilled in his deeds;
> I shall follow his footsteps joylessly,
> For, father, handsome Kaca I love."[5]

This is all it takes to dispel the great man's lethargy, though of course he does not know that at this moment the ashes of Kaca are circulating through his digestive system. Working himself up, he realizes suddenly that these repeated disappearances of the disciple who lives with him are personal affronts perpetrated against him by his employers, the demons. And he begins to see something even more serious: if he does not react, will these demons not be making him their accomplice in the most dreadful crime of all, the killing of a brahmin? And so, calling him by name, he summons Kaca. Kaca, no doubt, has long since sensed the difficulty of his position; he does not wish to kill his master as he did the wolves, and limits himself to announcing his presence in a soft voice. The master understands in turn, and exclaims (p. 178),

[5] The critical edition rejects the last two lines.

"Speak, brahmin! What path
Has brought you to lodge in this belly of mine?"

The youth replies:

"By your grace my memory survives:
I remember what has befallen and how.
Nor has my misery come to an end,
That I now must suffer this dismal pain.

The Asuras gave me to you in your wine
After killing and burning and grinding me, Kāvya.
But if you are there, can the Asura's magic
Prevail over a brahmin's wizardry?"

Under the circumstances, Devayānī's father thinks the decision should be referred to her:

"But how can I now do your wish, my daughter?
Kaca's life will murder me!
For but by opening my belly up
Can Kaca inside me appear, Devayānī."

A distant sister of Corneille's Chimène in *Le Cid*, Devayānī too recites her laments, condensed into one long couplet:

"Two sorrows burn me with heat of fire—
The death of Kaca and your destruction.
At Kaca's death I have no more shelter,
At your destruction I cannot live!"

Kāvya Uśanas ponders; there is only one way, a heroic one (pp. 178–179):

"Bṛhaspati's son, thou hast succeeded,
If Devayānī holds you so dear!
Then receive from me my life-giving magic,
If thou art not Indra in Kaca's guise.

No one can return from my belly and still live, bar one
brahmin.
Therefore receive thou my magic.

> I shall bear thee as a son, and thou
> Shalt bring me to life, from my body departed.
> Bestow thou the gracious look of the Law,
> When thou holdest the magic thy guru bestoweth!"

Everything turns out well, thanks to Kaca's loyalty (p. 179):

> Receiving the magic his guru bestowed
> And splitting his belly the brahmin came out,
> Did beautiful Kaca, from the brahmin's right side,
> As out of the bright weeks the moon rises full.
>
> And seeing him felled, a pile of learning,
> Did Kaca restore the dead man to life,
> Now that he possessed that magic lore;
> And Kaca saluted his guru and spoke.
>
> "Whoever pours the ambrosia of knowledge
> Into my ignorant ears as you have done,
> Him I consider both father and mother.
> Mindful of this deed, may I never become his enemy."[6]

Kaca's mission is accomplished, but of his promised thousand years of service, five hundred still remain. They come and go without incident, once Kāvya advises the demons that the only result of all their plotting was to force him to impart to his disciple the magic they had wanted to keep secret. When his contract is up, Kaca begs and is granted leave of his teacher, who apparently views calmly the passage of his secret into the service of the gods. It is with Devayānī that things go sour: she professes her love to the youth, makes much of the services rendered, and demands that he marry her. We shall return later to this unfortunate end to a thousand years of unblemished friendship. What is important here is that Kaca does not accede, and the two young people exchange curses instead of vows; the knowledge Kaca has acquired, Devayānī declares, he will be unable to use. "So be it," Kaca retorts,

[6] *yaḥ śrotrayoramṛtam saṃniṣiñcedyo me navidyasya yathā mamāyam tam manye 'haṃ pitaraṃ mātaram ca tasmai na druhyet kṛtamasya jānan*

"but those I will teach it to will use it!" As for Devayānī, avers Kaca, she will never wed a brahmin, a man of her own caste; if she ever marries she must become *déclassée*. Then he leaves and goes home to the gods, who give him the welcome he deserves (p. 181).

3. THE HUMILIATION AND SUBMISSION OF THE DEMONS

Devayānī could have saved her anger—once Kaca is gone, she shows no sign of grief, and he disappears from the story, and indeed from the whole epic, as he does from her heart. With him vanishes too the eternal conflict between the gods and the demons, having now been equalized. Besides, the girl wastes no time in finding trouble of another sort which will lead her devoted father to assertions and decisions loaded with consequences.

One day, she is bathing in a lake with Śarmiṣṭhā (the lovely daughter of Vṛṣaparvan, the king of the demons) and other companions. While they are in the water, the wind—or rather Indra transformed into the wind, a last and trifling form of the cosmic conflict—mixes up their clothing. When they get out, Śarmiṣṭhā innocently puts on Devayānī's dress. Thereupon follows a quarrel and a sharp exchange of words, the king's daughter saying in particular to the chaplain's (pp. 181–182):

> "Your father stands humbly below my father, whether he is sitting or lying, and he flatters and praises him constantly! You are the daughter of a man who must beg, flatter, and hold up his hand—I am the daughter of the one who gives, and does not receive, the one who is flattered."

When Devayānī tries to take back her dress by force, Śarmiṣṭhā throws her into a well (luckily a dry one), and calmly returns to her village: *Śarmiṣṭhā prākṣipat kūpe tataḥ svapuram avrajat*. A *kṣatriya* out hunting discovers the poor girl: It is Nahuṣa's son, King Yayāti, whom we will meet again soon, for this rescue will have strange consequences. She holds out her right hand to him, he pulls her out of the well and goes on his way. Imagine Devayānī's state of mind! She dispatches to her father the first woman she sees, ordering her to tell him what has happened. As for her, after this insult, she refuses to set foot again in the city of the king of the demons. Her father hastens out, and at first he tries to reason with her: all the unpleasantnesses that befall us, he says, are the results of our own faults, and probably she is being punished for something. Devayānī rejects the argument. Punishment or no, she says, "Listen to the words I had to put up with from the mouth of Śarmiṣṭhā, Vṛṣaparvan's daughter" (p. 183):

> "What she said was that you are the songster of the Daityas! That is what Śarmiṣṭhā told me, her eyes bloodshot with rage, in the harshest and sharpest words, 'You are the daughter of a man who must beg, flatter, and hold up his hand—I am the daughter of the one who gives, and does not receive, the one who is flattered.' That is what Śarmiṣṭhā again and again said to me, Vṛṣaparvan's daughter, eyes red with fury, swollen with pride. Father, if I am the daughter of a man who flatters and holds up his hand, I shall seek her good graces; so I told my friend."

The reaction is immediate and complete. The father is wounded in his priestly, or rather magicianly, honor:

> "You are *not* the daughter of a flattering beggar who holds up his hand, my dear! You are the daughter, Devayānī, of the one who is praised but does not praise. Vṛṣaparvan himself knows it, and Indra, and King Yayāti. Inconceivable Brahman beyond compare is my sovereign strength!
>
> Whatsoever is on earth or in heaven, I am its master forever, Brahma was delighted and told me this. I set loose the water, in my care for all creatures, I feed all growing things; I tell you the truth!"[7]

[7] The Poona edition rejects the last two *ślokas*:

yac ca kiṃcit sarvagataṃ bhūmau vā yadi vā divi
tasyāham īśvaro nityaṃ tuṣṭenoktaḥ svayaṃbhuvā.
ahaṃ jalaṃ vimuñcāmi prajānāṃ hitakāmyayā
puṣṇāmy auṣadhayaḥ sarvā iti satyaṃ bravīmi te.

After consoling his daughter with this blustering revelation, he goes on to give her an ineffectual lecture on patience. She insists that she will not go on living in a place where she has been humiliated—she would rather die. Thus Kāvya goes to the king of the demons and announces his well-founded resolve; the injury of his daughter on top of the murder of his innocent student—this is too much! (p. 184):

> "I, Vṛṣaparvan, listen to me, shall forsake you and your kin. I cannot dwell with you any longer in your domain, king."

The king begs his pardon: if Kāvya abandons them and leaves their country, the demons will have no choice but to take refuge in the ocean. A most interesting dialogue follows:

> "Drown in the ocean or run to the horizons, Asuras! I cannot suffer any unkindness done to my daughter, for I love her. Make your peace with Devayānī, with whom my life is lodged. I am your only safeguard, as Bṛhaspati is Indra's."
>
> "Whatever riches can be found with the lords of the Asuras, Bhārgava, whatever wealth on earth of elephants, horses, and cows, you own it as you own me!"
>
> "Whatever wealth the lords of the Daityas own, grand Asuras, I own it only if you make your peace with Devayānī."

Vṛṣaparvan capitulates unconditionally. Kāvya goes to report to his daughter, who is still not satisfied:

> "If you, father, . . . say you own all the wealth of the king and the king himself, I won't believe it from you. Let the king say it himself!"

Vṛṣaparvan promises:

> "Whatever desire you desire, sweet-smiling Devayānī, I shall give it to you with both hands, however hard it may be to find."
>
> "I want Śarmiṣṭhā as my slave, with a thousand handmaidens. And after me shall she follow wherever my father will marry me!"

Vṛṣaparvan does not even answer, but sends the nurse to hurry and fetch Śarmiṣṭhā, who does not argue any more. With her retinue, she goes to give herself up to her new mistress, suffering a last insult with dignity (p. 185):

> "With a thousand maidens I am your slave to serve you. And after you shall I follow wherever your father marries you."
>
> "Am I the daughter of a songster who flatters and holds up his hand? How is it that the daughter of the man who is flattered will be my slave?"
>
> "Whatever the way, I want to bring luck to my suffering kinsmen. So I shall follow after you, wherever your father will marry you."

Only now does Devayānī decide to go back to the city. She tells her father:

> "Now will I enter the castle, father. I am pleased, greatest of the twiceborn. Your knowledge is unfailing, and so is the power of your magic."

4. THE AGING AND REJUVENATION OF YAYĀTI

The redoubtable young lady had no idea that this excessive redress would lead to a still more humiliating trial for her. Later on we shall examine it from King Yayāti's perspective; for now let us consider it only insofar as it sheds light on the character of Kāvya Uśanas.

Kaca, by his counter-curse, had condemned Devayānī never to marry a brahmin; and as for King Yayāti, in order to pull her out of the well, he had taken her hand, a saving gesture, but one that could also be taken as a sign of engagement. Consequently, when she encounters him again hunting in the same forest, while she is out playing with Śarmiṣṭhā and her companions, she demands that he marry her. The king is less than eager. In fact he seems to be most interested in the gracious Śarmiṣṭhā, and is astonished that the daughter of a king is in a position of slavery. He claims that, being a kṣatriya, he cannot marry a brahmin's daughter, especially the daughter of the great Kāvya Uśanas—mixing classes is a sin, and the anger of brahmins is like a deadly poisonous snake. She answers that there are precedents for such unions, and in both directions; if he is afraid to marry her without her father's permission, let him just wait. She sends a messenger to Uśanas, who rushes out and takes care of everything: he gives away (or inflicts) his daughter, and with the authority of a dharma master, exempts the kṣatriya from the matrimonial interdiction (p. 187). Then he concludes:

> "Marry the slim-waisted Devayānī by the Law, and with her you shall find happiness beyond compare! This young maiden too you should always respect, king, this Śarmiṣṭhā, daughter of Vṛṣaparvan, and never call her to your bed."

Reassured, Yayāti takes leave of his father-in-law and takes his new wife Devayānī back to his city, along with Śarmiṣṭhā and their two thousand followers.

The stage is all set. Yayāti has two children by his wife, and secretly, three by the servant princess. Not that he failed to put up any resistance; but in addition to her beauty, Śarmiṣṭhā is able to muster up three more reasons in quick succession. They surprise us, but they persuade him: (1) a woman's husband is really also the spouse of his wife's friends, (2) any man owes it to any woman to save her from the misfortune of childlessness when, at the proper time, she asks for his help, and (3) in his capacity as husband, Yayāti is the master of Devayānī, who is Śarmiṣṭhā's mistress; therefore he is also the master of Śarmiṣṭhā.

One day the inevitable happens. While the royal couple—the official one—are out walking on the grounds, Śarmiṣṭhā's sons heedlessly throw themselves around Yayāti's neck and call him "Daddy." Offended, Devayānī goes back to her father (p. 190).

Yayāti follows her, but before he can speak, Kāvya Uśanas condemns and sentences him (p. 191):

> "Great king, since you who know the Law have broken the Law for your pleasure, invincible decrepitude shall ravage you this instant!"

The unfortunate king pleads with him. Of the three reasons Śarmiṣṭhā used to convince him, he mentions only the best one, the second, which makes adultery not a right but a duty. His father-in-law has no trouble answering this with another duty, the more serious as it puts Yayāti under obligation not to Devayānī, but to him, Kāvya Uśanas, who had expressly forbidden him to call Śarmiṣṭhā to his bed:

> "Should I not have been consulted? You are my dependent, king. Duplicity in matters of Law makes one a thief, Nāhuṣa!"

The result:

> So it befell that Uśanas in anger cursed Yayāti Nāhuṣa. And he lost his previous youth and fell instantly to senility.

He still has the presence of mind to suggest that he is not alone in being punished:

> "I am unsated of my youth on Devayānī, scion of the Bhṛgu. Show me grace, brahmin; do not let old age lay hold of me!"
>
> "Such things I do not say idly. You have reached old age, king of the earth. But if you wish, you may pass your old age to another."
>
> "Share in my kingdom, share in my merit, share in my fame shall the son who will give me his youth; brahmin, consent to that!"
>
> "You shall pass on your old age, as you wish, son of Nahuṣa, if you call me to your mind. Then you will reap no evil. The son who will give you his youth shall become the king, long-lived, famous, and rich in offspring."

Once he returns to his city, it is not easy for Yayāti to rid himself of his misfortune. He endures the complete, flat refusal of his first four sons. Only the fifth, Pūru, sacrifices himself (p. 193).[8] As for the procedure, it is so simple it will make many a septuagenarian daydream:

> Then much-suffering Yayāti, calling Kāvya to his mind, transferred his old age to his magnanimous son.[9]

Being reasonable, he has asked this sacrifice of Pūru for only a short thousand years. He takes care to make good use of them, never failing in his religious duties. In the absence of Devayānī, of whom there is no further mention, a celestial young lady, an Apsaras, kindly helps him, and not only in performing his more austere duties. When the thousand years are up, having realized the vanity of worldly pleasures, he restores Pūru's youth to him, gives him the throne, retires to the forest, dies, and ascends to heaven. His post-mortem adventures are dealt with in *The Destiny of a King*; Kāvya Uśanas is not involved in those.

[8] See *The Destiny of a King* (Chicago, 1973), chapter 1.

[9] *evam uktvā yayātis tu kāvyaṃ smṛtvā mahātapāḥ*
saṃkrāmayām āsa jarāṃ tadā pūrau mahātmani

III

THE KAVI, THE GODS, AND THE DEMONS

1. THE ANCIENT MEANING OF KAVÍ

The sequence of episodes that we have just read can tell us a great many things regarding Kāvya Uśanas, but they must be preceded by a correction which has already been mentioned briefly.

In the social world of the *Mahābhārata*, dominated by the system of varṇas—brahmins, kṣatriyas, and vaiśyas—the character of Kāvya Uśanas was formed as far as possible on the general model of the brahmin. He is presented as the opposite number of Bṛhaspati: one is the chaplain of the demons, the other of the gods. Even his relationships with the king of the demons are for the most part simply amplified versions of the usual ones between a king and his chaplain: one pays to be praised, the other is paid for praising. But the king also surrounds the priest with a respect that the latter repays by providing mystical aid for him and his subjects, in the rural economy as well as in war, by facilitating the rain and the growth of plants as well as by ensuring success on the battlefield. Still, the *Mahābhārata* cannot make this brahmin completely like all the rest. Kāvya Uśanas, it seems, serves the king of the demons less by the everyday celebration of liturgies than by his awesome and unmatched ability to resurrect the dead; that is, more as a magician than a priest. The poem introduces him as the son of Bhṛgu, himself the son of Varuṇa, and this puts him in a strong position in relation to his colleague and rival Bṛhaspati: whereas the brahmins, like their abstract principle, the *bráhman*, normally belong to Mitra, as we learn from the *Śatapatha-Brāhmaṇa*[1] and many other texts, Kāvya Uśanas is as it were a "Varuṇian brahmin," that is, in a word, a great magician. But in Vedic times, the difference was more important: a kaví or "son of kaví" was surely something other than a simple priest.

In the *Journal Asiatique* (1953),[2] Louis Renou gave a brief but substantial sketch. "The performer of ritual, by deed and word," he says first of all, and he defines the abstract noun *kā́vya* as the "know-how" which takes charge of the sacrifice: thus Agni, often called kaví as well as hótar, "possesses all the kā́vyas (*ṚgVeda* 2.5.3) because he takes care of all the steps conducive to the success of the sacrifice." This could refer to any priest who knows his business. But the knowledge of the kaví goes beyond ordinary technical operations, or at least directs them from a higher level:

> One questions the kaví "to get knowledge": in *RV* 7.8.3, the author wants to know why Varuṇa stands aloof from mankind. He asks those who understand (*cikitvás*), and these, expressly identified as kavís, tell him unanimously . . . [the answer follows]. "Who can say, proving himself (thus) to be a kaví [asks the author of 1.164.18, a hymn with cosmogonic riddles], whence divine thought was born?" The author of 3.38.1 calls the kavís to witness his speech in order to question them, and through them to sound the origins of the cosmos. The Kavi (or Kāvya, "son of kavi") above all others is Uśanas (the maker of Indra's thunderbolt [1.51.10]; gatherer of herds [1.83.5]; etc.), who utters oracles (1.174.7); another is Kutsa, who has reached the status of a demigod. In short, the kaví is he who is consulted precisely because he is a kaví, any further definition being useless: *tā́* (Indra and Agni) *u kavitvanā́ kavī́ pṛcchyámānā* (8.40.3).

[1] 4.1.4.2.
[2] Vol. 241: 180–183.

But it is not by chance that the *ṚgVeda*, in the few passages where it mentions him, denotes his activity by the verb *takṣ-*, "to fashion," which elsewhere applies to the divine craftsmen, Tvaṣṭar or the Ṛbhus: his "knowledge" allows him, besides his normal role in the sacrifice, to "create." "The activity of the kaví," to quote Renou again, "is often not so different from *māyā́*, the power which 'modifies' and 'changes' the rational appearance of things."

In short, if the kaví has a patron among the sovereign gods, it is less Mitra, who is closer to the sacrificing priests, than Varuṇa, whom 5.13.1 calls *diváḥ kavíḥ*, "the kavi of heaven."

In the *ṚgVeda*, as we have seen, Kāvya Uśanas is on good terms with the gods, but he is not their chaplain, and he does not live among them: Indra comes to visit him "from afar," in order to acquire the means for an exploit. In sum, he mythically represents, at the fringe of the gods and the demons, a third type of powerful being, one whose support is solicited by both sides and given to one side or the other, but which can also be withheld; and without his being truly committed by either sentiment or necessity to the side he supports. As early as Vedic prose literature we find him in the service of the demons, but he maintains ties to the gods which, if he were not so quintessentially independent, would amount to sheer betrayal of his employers: *Tāṇḍya Brāhmaṇa* 7.5.20 says explicitly that he lets himself be corrupted by the gods, *upāmantrayanta*.[3] In the story of the first book of the *Mahābhārata* which we have just analyzed, he seems closer to Bṛhaspati, the chaplain of the gods, than to the demons he serves. The war notwithstanding, he takes on Bṛhaspati's son as his disciple and protects him against the demons, who on good grounds are shocked and disturbed by this enemy presence, and in the end he passes to him the secret that until then, through him alone, ensured the superiority of the demons. It certainly is possible, let us note in passing, that at the secular level such a type of holy man—he is no more than this in India, and probably still in the *gāthās* of Zarathuštra (unless the

[3] Pischel, *Vedische Studien* II: 167.

kavis there are not already, as is generally thought, petty rulers inimical to the new religion)[4]—was able to attain elsewhere, in eastern Iran, some political power.

In the comparison of Kāvya Uśanas and Kavi Usan, we should not lose sight of this twofold evolution from a single more archaic type—the far-reaching though incomplete "brahminization" of the first versus the almost total "secularization" of the second. With this caution in mind, let us examine the three episodes of the story in the *Mahābhārata* (sections 2, 3, and 4 in Chapter 2 above), starting with the second episode (section 3).

2. THE WEALTH OF KĀVYA UŚANAS AND KAY ŪS

Every brahmin is, rightfully, greater than the king whom he serves: the very name of the chaplain, puróhita, undoubtedly

[4] Two meanings, or at least two interpretations, are generally acknowledged for the Iranian title *kavi*: (1) in the *Gāthās*, it designates a class of leaders of whom Zarathuštra speaks ill because they practice the cults against which his reform is directed; (2) later it is the name of a dynasty of which the Zoroastrians speak well because Vištāspa, one of the last holders of the title, converted to the True Religion. Various ways have been suggested of reconciling at least the first of these with the Vedic value: "sorcerer princes" (Jacques Duchesne-Guillemin), "sacral tribal chieftains (*sakrale Stammefyrster*)" (Kaj Barr). Ilya Gershevitch, *The Avestan Hymn to Mithra* (Cambridge, 1959), p. 185, has gone further: first, he says, "in the Gāthic *kavis*, mentioned on a par with *karapans* and *usigs*, who are agreed to have been respective members of two priestly classes, we may as well recognize the Iranian counterparts of the Vedic *kavis*: composers of hymns to various gods, who in addition had perhaps assumed certain priestly functions; they would incur Zarathuštra's disapproval because of their insistence on the traditional Indo-Iranian ritual." Second, "one particular family of *kavis*, whose home was in Sīstān, rose to temporal power and came to rule over the Khorasmian state or part of it; this family used the professional designation *kavi* as a personal dynastic surname. Zarathuštra, in addressing his protector as *Kavi Vištāspa*, would not associate the king's dynastic name with the class-name of the priestly hymn-writers . . . any more than we are apt to think of parsons when addressing Mr. John Parson." This reconstruction, right from the start, deprives the Vedic kaví of his essential importance as a "free magician" by reducing him to a kind of priest (when *ṚgVeda* 3.2.4 calls Agni *uśíjaṃ*

means nothing less than he who is "placed before," and a famous stanza in the seventh book of the *ṚgVeda* states this claim in so many words. In practice, chaplain and king, and more generally brahmin and kṣatriya, observe a modus vivendi that is always perfectly honorable as far as the priest is concerned, but less limiting for the man of action. The second episode of the story of Kāvya Uśanas ends in something entirely different: a surrender of the demons and their king as total as that demanded of defeated peoples by the conquering Romans. The king recognizes Kāvya Uśanas as his master, his daughter becomes the slave of Uśanas's daughter, and all the wealth of the people, of the nobles in particular, is forfeit to Uśanas. If the holy man wished, he could become the king of the demons himself, removing Vṛṣaparvan and becoming the exact equivalent of a Kayanid. He prefers to keep his status as an outsider, but what spoils! Let us reread the terms of the hapless king's surrender:[5]

> "Whatever riches can be found with the lords of the Asuras, Bhārgava, whatever wealth on earth of elephants, horses, and cows, you own it as you own me!"

This is not just a polite turn of phrase, as when a shopkeeper in an Eastern bazaar receives an unknown visitor by saying to him: "My store is all yours." Vṛṣaparvan is in no position to dicker. And we know from elsewhere that Uśanas is wealth-prone. The story in the first book, being more concerned with Devayānī and the enslavement of Śarmiṣṭhā, does not stress this point, even at the moment of the demon king's capitulation; but in the sixth

kavíkratum, this does not put *uśíj* "on a par" with kaví; Agni is a priest, seer, and sorcerer all at once. In the first place, the hypothesis does not take into consideration the equivalence of the Gāthic kavis to the *dušəxšaϑrā dahyunąm*, "bad rulers of countries" (*Yasna* 48, 10); in the second place, it assumes a secularization of religious matters and titles hardly admissible in such societies. In the Manichean literature, *kavān* is used in the sense of "giants"; see Arthur Christensen, *L'Iran sous les Sassanides* (Copenhagen, 1936), p. 193 and n. 4.

[5] Above, p. 36.

book the legendary wealth of Uśanas inspires the admiration of onlookers:[6]

> "On its peak [viz., Meru, the mythical mountain] in the sky is Uśanas Kāvya, O King. Golden jewels are his, his too are mountains of treasure. Divine Kubera [god of wealth] receives from him a quarter of it; of that wealth he gives a sixteenth to men."

This picture of the demons yielding to Kāvya Uśanas as their lord and master, *īśvara*, and the other image of Uśanas seated high in the sky on the summit of the mythical mountain, master of three times more wealth than the god who specializes in it, are close to those that the Middle Iranian texts and the epic of the Islamic period provide about the king who is his homonym. Already in *Yašt* 5, 45–47, we read that Kavi Usan attained "to the highest power over all lands, over men and over the demons." But the *Dēnkart* and the *Bundahišn*, following passages of the Sassanian *Avesta*, are more precise. Arthur Christensen, over fifty years ago, collected what they had to say:[7]

> In the midst of the Elburz mountains, according to the *Sūtkar Nask*, Kay Ūs had built seven abodes, one of gold, two of silver, two of steel, and two of crystal, and from this fortress he kept a tight rein on the Mazanian demons and prevented them from destroying the world. . . . This feature is found also in the chapter of the Iranian *Bundahišn* which describes the dwellings erected by the Kayanids. It is reported there that the abode of Kay Ūs was comprised of a house of

[6] Śl. 217–218 (Nīlakaṇṭha understands the two *tasyas* of the second line in this way):

tasyaiva mūrddhany uśanāḥ kāvyo divi mahīpate
haimāni tasya ratnāni tasyaite ratnaparvatāḥ
tasmāt kubero bhagavāṃś caturthaṃ bhāgam aśnute.
tataḥ kalāṃśaṃ vittasya manuṣyebhyaḥ prayacchati.

[7] *Les Kayanides*, p. 74; Madan (ed.), *Dēnkart* 9.22.4, p. 815; *Zand-Ākāsīh, Iranian or Greater Bundahisn*, 32.11, ed. and trans. by Behramgore Tehmuras Anklesaria (Bombay, 1956), p. 270, trans. p. 271.

gold, in which he lived himself, two of crystal which were the stables for his horses, and two of steel for his flocks.

Except for the elephants, these are the same treasures that the demons handed over to Kāvya Uśanas, or that he amassed on the summit of Mount Meru. Later, Firdausi, the lavish Persian inheritor of the Zoroastrian tradition, said in his *Book of Kings*,[8]

> Everyone was small before Kaūs, and those who wore crowns formed his retinue. . . . He built a residence on Mount Elburz and wore out the dīvs by this work. He ordered them to cut into the cliffs and to construct two palaces on top of them, each ten versts across. He had stables hewn in the rock where all the bars were of steel, all the pillars of hard stone, and to them were tied his war horses and his dromedaries for racing and carrying. He built a palace of crystal which he incrusted with emeralds: this was the venue of his festivals and feasts, the place where he took the nourishment that sustained his body. He set up a cupola of onyx from Yemen in which a Mobad of high renown had to live; he had this edifice built so that knowledge would never leave this place. Thereafter he constructed two more of them to house his weapons, and he built them with silver ingots. Finally he erected a palace of gold to live in. It was one hundred twenty palms high, covered with figures encrusted with turquoises, with a reception hall decorated with rubies. . . . The dīvs were so worn out by these labors that they could no longer do evil. Ill fortune lay dormant, so great were the goodness and justice of the master who chained the dīvs up by his works and afflicted them by his punishments.

With minor variations and the intervention of Salomon, another famous demon tamer, the motif appears in Belᶜamī:[9]

> Kay Kaūs asked that Salomon put the dīvs under his command. Salomon granted his request, and Kay Kaūs had

[8] J. Mohl (ed.), *Le Livre des Rois* II: 40–41.
[9] Zotenberg, *Chronique de Tabarī* I: 465.

the dīvs construct a city of seventy parasangs in length which he named Kenkeret, or Qairūn according to others. He ordered them to encircle it with a wall of iron, another of copper, a third of silver, and a fourth of gold. He collected whatever of value he owned and all his treasures in this city and entrusted them to the protection of the dīvs.

Al-Thaᶜālibī's geography is more precise:[10]

> Kay Kaūs, when God had raised his fame and prestige very high, had placed under his power all the regions and the greatest of his servants, and had caused him to acquire an opulence the like of which had never been known among his predecessors, established his residence in Iraq and had constructed in Babylon that high tower that contained compartments of stone, iron, brass, copper, lead, silver, and gold, and presents and tribute were brought to him from Rum, India, and China.

Christensen, who had refused a priori to take the Indic Kāvya Uśanas into consideration, wrote in this regard:[11]

> All that the Middle Iranian books have to say relating to Kay Ūs, apart from the scanty accounts drawn from the Yašts, represents without any doubt a new layer in the evolution of the tradition; for the substance of the story of this king, which we have just sketched, is obviously an imitation of the story of Yim. . . . This imitated pattern has been modified and amplified by all sorts of motifs and features of diverse origins. In the seven dwellings constructed of exotic and precious materials (gold, silver, steel, crystal [according to the Middle Iranian texts]), we have a very old legendary motif that has been perpetuated through the centuries in popular stories and legends. It goes back ultimately to the seven colors of the planets used

[10] *Histoire des Rois des Perses*, ed. and trans. Hermann Zotenberg (1900 [photographic reedition, Teheran, 1963]), p. 165.

[11] *Les Kayanides*, pp. 79–81.

in the construction of Babylonian temples. Herodotus, describing the fortress of Ecbatana (I, 98), which he attributes to Deiokes, informs us that the concentric ramparts had battlements painted in seven colors; they were white, black, purple, blue, pink, silver, and gold, respectively.

It is in fact probable that this traditional Babylonian description has helped to formulate the manner in which Kavi Usa(δa)n, master of the demons, made them safeguard unprecedented wealth on the mythical Mount Elburz (and later in Babylon itself). But the Indic Kāvya Uśanas, receiving from the conquered demons ownership of all their goods, and sitting enthroned on the peak of Mount Meru, in possession of three-fourths of all the gold and jewels in the world, vouchsafes that, alongside the Yašts and despite their silence, this feature descends from a genuine Indo-Iranian tradition. It does not belong to a "new layer"; far from being an "amplification" of the "imitated pattern," it is the Indo-Iranian tradition that guided the amplifiers in search of models of wealth toward the skyscrapers of Babylon.

The Babylonian depiction, let it be said in passing, has been curiously Iranianized. Except in al-Thaʿālibī, the planetary number seven that it involved appears curtailed in various ways, and combined with another more reduced classification that is none other than that of the three Indo-European functions. The most complete structure is that of Firdausi, where after the mention of the stables hewn in the rock the buildings are enumerated: the palace of crystal and emeralds for food; the onyx cupola for the mobad and learning; the two buildings of silver for weapons; and finally the palace of gold, turquoise, and rubies as the royal residence. Thus, as well as the fairy realm in which he lived and wielded his power, Kaūs had within arm's reach, in separate places, his weapons, his priest-scholar, and his victuals. It is likely that the same classification explains the reduction of the seven palaces to five in the *Bundahišn*: the royal residence in gold, two stables of crystal for the horses, and two cattle sheds of steel for the flocks.

3. KAY ŪS, THE DEMONS AND GOD

Most of the Pahlavi or Persian texts that have just been cited see in this wealth and in the edifices that embodied it a mark of divine favor, and in the enslavement of the demons a pious work, useful to the good creation. The only exception is Belʿamī, who expressly says that God took a dim view of the construction of the city of "Kenkeret"; after telling how the king "stockpiled in this city his treasures and all the precious things he possessed, and consigned them to the care of dīvs," he adds:[12]

> God sent several angels from heaven to destroy this town and its walls. Kay Kaūs ordered the dīvs to oppose them. But the dīvs could not save it. Kay Kaūs was incensed with them and killed all their chiefs. . . . After the destruction of the city, he grew sad and said: "It is absolutely necessary that I ascend to heaven and see the sky, the stars, the sun and the moon. . . ."

More usually, it is not God who initiates the hostilities. It is Kay Ūs himself, in a natural surge of arrogance or inspired by some devil; alone or at the head of the army of the demons who are subject to him, he undertakes to ascend to heaven, and not with the honest curiosity of an explorer, but as a conqueror. Here is Christensen's discussion:[13]

> The dīvs plotted the ruin of Kay Ūs, reports the *Dēnkart*, IX, 22, 5–7, following the *Sūtkar Nask*. Then Xēšm (Aēšma), the demon of bloody cruelty, went to him and corrupted his soul, so that he was not content with the possession of the seven *kišvars*, or parts of the world; aspiring to rule over heaven and the abodes of the Amahrspands (Aməša Spəntas, the Zoroastrian archangels), he began to make war against God and offended him. . . . With an army of demons and

[12] *Chronique de Tabarī* I: 465.

[13] *Les Kayanides*, pp. 75, 78. It is this tradition, distorted, which resulted in Theodore bar Kōnay's peculiar note: "Kikaouz was a mountain ram who butted the sky with his horns" (Christensen, *L'Iran sous les Sassanides*, p. 151).

evil-doers, the text goes on, he launches himself from the peak of Mount Elburz up to the last frontier between darkness and the celestial light, where the Glory of the Kayanids (*kavaem* x^{v}*arənah*) stands in the form [of a boundary stone] of clay (?). Once, he is separated from his army, but he does not give up and renews the attack. Then the Creator recalls from him the Glory of the Kayanids; the army of Kay Ūs falls to earth from this height and Kay Ūs himself flees into the sea of Vourukaša.

Most often, the scene is imagined differently, following patterns that Christensen has well identified:[14]

> According to another tradition, Kay Ūs started from his palace, rising in the air by means of a magic machine (Belᶜamī), or a seat or a box carried by trained eagles or vultures, lured by pieces of meat suspended from spears to which the birds were attached (Dīnawarī, Thaᶜālibī, Firdausi); the last feature, borrowed from the Alexander Romance, goes back ultimately to the Babylonian legend of Etana.

The most moving version of the narrative is Firdausi's:[15]

> Now it happened one morning that Iblīs held an assembly, unbeknownst to the king, and said to the dīvs: "The king makes our lives painful and hard these days. Some cunning dīv, knowing the customs and the ways of the palace, will have to approach Kaūs and turn his soul aside from the true path, in order to deliver the dīvs from their misery, in order to estrange the king's spirit from God the Very Pure and spread dust over his shining glory." The dīvs listened to his words and pondered. But none dared to speak, because they were afraid of Kaūs. At last, one dīv full of wickedness stood up saying: "I am the one who will take on this hard task; I will turn Kaūs away from the service of God. . . ."

The king is only too quick to lend an ear to the diabolical adviser, and in the end decides to exalt himself to the highest of the

[14] *Les Kayanides,* pp. 109–110.
[15] *Le Livre des Rois* II: 43–51.

heavens. To do so, he has to raise with particular care four powerful eaglets.

> When these eaglets had become as strong as lions, so that they could carry off a wild sheep, the king had constructed a wooden throne from Indian aloe, which was reinforced by gold plates. Then at the sides of the throne long javelins were attached. All being thus prepared, and his entire soul absorbed in this desire, he suspended from these javelins quarters of mutton. Last, he had the four strong eagles brought in and attached them firmly to the throne. Kaūs sat on the throne, setting before him a cup of wine; and the mighty-winged eagles, stirred by hunger, hurled themselves toward the pieces of meat. They raised the throne off the ground, carried it from the earth toward the clouds, and turned their efforts to the pieces of meat, as long as strength remained in them. I have heard it said that Kaūs reached a point just above the firmament and that he continued in the hope of raising himself above the angels; another says that he had flown toward heaven in order to fight it with bow and arrows.[16] On this point there are all sorts of traditions, but the truth is known only by the One who has wisdom. The eagles flew for a long time, then stopped: such will be the fate of those who would attempt this enterprise. But when the birds were exhausted, they became discouraged, folded their wings after their habit, and descended from the dark clouds, pulling after them the javelins and the king's throne. They headed for a forest and landed near Amol. Miraculously, the shock of hitting the ground did not kill the king, and what was to happen still remained a secret. The king wished that a wild duck would take flight, because he needed to eat a little. Thus, he had exchanged his power and his throne for shame and punishment. He stayed in the forest completely exhausted and addressed his prayers to God the Creator.

[16] *šinīd-am ki kāvūs šud bar falak*
hamī raft tā bar šav-ad bar malak
digar guft az ān raft bar āsmān
ki tā ǰang sāz-ad bi tīr u kamān

The Islamic poet says that the king prayed to God and, in the end, God pardoned him:

> While Kaūs thus begged God's mercy for his sins, his army searched everywhere for him. Finally Rustam, Gīv, and Tūs received news of him and went off with an army, complete with elephants and kettledrums. The old Gūdarz said to Rustam: "Since my mother nourished me with milk, I have seen in this world many crowns and thrones, many kings and grandees over whom fortuned smiled. But never have I seen, neither among the humble nor among the great, a man as obstinate as Kaūs. He has neither sense, wisdom, nor prudence; he has neither the right spirit nor his heart in the right place. You could say that he does not have brains in his head, and not a single one of his thoughts is good. Never has any grandee of the past made an attempt against heaven. But Kaūs is like a man possessed, without direction or reason, and each wind that blows carries him away."[17] Then the Pahlavāns came near him, full of bitterness and anger; they reproached him, and Gūdarz said to him: "A hospital would be a more suitable place for you than a palace. Constantly you abandon your throne to your enemies, without ever disclosing to anyone your insane plans. Three times you have fallen into misfortune and calamity, without your spirit becoming any wiser by these trials. You led your army into the Māzandarān: remember how many misfortunes resulted from that! Another time you made yourself the guest of your enemy, and from his idol you became his servant. There remained in the world none but God the All Pure who did not request his investiture upon your sword. You traversed the earth in order to subdue it, and now you are declaring war on heaven. If you raise yourself a hand's breadth higher than you should, you are wholly in revolt against God. You have always found a way to extricate yourself from misfortune, but after your death people will say that there was a king who wanted to climb to heaven to see the moon and the sun, and to count the stars

[17] This last development is not retained in Bertel's' critical edition.

one by one. Behave like sensible, good, and pious kings. With all your strength strive only for submission to God, and whether in happiness or in misfortune, beseech him alone."

Kaūs was abashed and ate up the shame with which the great and worthy ones covered him. At the end he answered: "Justice cannot suffer from what is true. All you have said is true and fair, and my soul is a prisoner of your snares." From his eyes flowed tears of bile, and he uttered many prayers to the Creator. Thereupon he picked up his weapons and got into a litter, weighed down by remorse and sadness. When he arrived at his palace and in front of his raised throne, he remained burdened by what had happened. For forty days he stood respectfully before God, measuring the ground with his body and leaving his throne empty. In his shame, he did not dare to go out of his palace: it could have been said that he was going to wear his skin out. He shed tears of blood while praying and asking forgiveness from God the guide. His pride having been curbed by the shame that he experienced in front of these worthies, he abstained from festivals and kept the door of his audience hall closed. He repented and lost himself in his sorrow and his cares; he gave away the great treasures he had amassed and rubbed his cheek against the black earth, imploring God the All Pure.

Having thus spent some time in tears, he obtained his forgiveness from the Creator, and from everywhere the warriors who had scattered regrouped around his throne. Then he shone anew by the grace of God. He understood that his penance was over. He sat on the golden throne, the crown on his head, and opened the door of a treasure-house to the army. He rejuvenated the whole world, himself shining above the great and the humble: one could have said that as a result of his justice the earth became a brocade, and the king of kings sat majestically on his throne.

In an Islamic setting, the old Zoroastrian tradition persists, both as regards the moral instability of this king, who is neither completely good nor wholly bad,[18] and also as to his relationship

[18] Cf. Al-Thaʿālibī, *Histoire des Rois des Perses*, pp. 154–155, describing the character of Kay Kaūs: "K. had an astonishing character, extremely unstable: some-

with God, with its oscillation between service and rebellion, punishment and mercy. The Pahlavi books multiply the reports of the sins of Kay Ūs against justice and the men of God, and it is sometimes possible to determine from where these accounts come, but their conjunction in itself is instructive. And yet Kay Ūs is not treated as strictly, as irremediably by God as is Yim, for instance, who was guilty of a single and unique fit of pride. He is allowed the chance to repent, and although he loses his privileges (immortality, in certain Middle Iranian texts) and suffers setbacks in reprisal, in the end he can pass the kingship on honorably to his grandson and die at peace with men and heaven.

This ambiguity that marks the character, the behavior, and the fate of Kavi Usan corresponds, in monotheistic Iran, to what in India is simply the freedom of action, flexibility, and oscillation of Kāvya Uśanas between the gods and the demons. On this point, Vedic and epic India has undoubtedly stayed closer to the Indo-Iranian state of affairs, which the Zoroastrian reform profoundly modified. In India, the demons and the gods are two peoples at war; both are honorable in certain respects (the translation "demon" is misleading), and although the ordinary man, lacking power of his own, has an interest in choosing the side of the gods, nourishing and soliciting them regularly through cultic acts, the mythical kavís, with their very powerful knowledge, were in a position to maintain their autonomy between the two sides. As was noted above, they can intervene without becoming completely involved, and thus set a high price on this limited and revocable assistance. Zoroastrian Iran allows no one a position between good and evil, and admits neither neutrality nor subtlety—the choice, the theme of one of the most important gāthās, must be frank, total, and irrevocable; every man, every being, is either *ašavant* or *drəgvant*, adhering entirely either to the true Order or to the Lie, to

times a good ruler, sometimes a violent tyrant; one day an irreproachable king, the next a rebellious Satan; at times serious and prudent, at other times fickle and thoughtless. . . . He ruled with these diversions: his character laid him low and his good fortune raised him again; his decisions ruined him and his lucky star saved him."

Ōhrmazd or to Ahriman. No more than any of the kavi kings can Kay Ūs escape this necessity, and by attacking God, even though only once, by rising up against him at the head of the dīvs, he calls upon himself sanctions that can never be reversed. And yet here is the miracle: to him alone, in the Iranian saga, Ōhrmazd gives forgiveness and grants favor. Why? Aside from a rather interesting novelistic explanation, to which we shall return, the answer is simple: the Indo-Iranian theme of the free and thus variable relationship of the kavi—the holy man—to the gods and the demons was forced, in the Zoroastrian ideology, to produce the extended career of a kavi—a temporal king—now saint and now sinner, the object now of God's protection, now of his anger, but also his forgiveness: the repeated forgiveness without which he could not have persisted in this scandalous behavior that defined him.

IV

THE POWER OF THE KAVI

1. THE POWER OF RESURRECTION IN BATTLES BETWEEN GODS AND DEMONS

The independence of Kāvya Uśanas between gods and demons and Kavi Usan's fluctuation between God and the demons having thus been recognized as parallel, let us examine the actions of each—that is, in terms of Kāvya Uśanas, the first and then third episodes of his story (i.e., the resuscitation of Kaca and the aging of Yayāti).

Wars between demons and gods and their epic derivatives or their "historical" substitutes, occasionally entail in the Indo-European world an element comparable to the one that dominates the first episode of this story: one of the two parties possesses a technique, material or formulaic, either to revive the dead or to assure the invulnerability and immortality of its combatants, and the other side seeks to get hold of this technique or to destroy it.

Thus, in Irish legend, in the decisive battle of Moytura which pits the Túatha Dé Danann, "the people of the goddess Dana"—that is to say, the ancient Celtic gods—against the demonic Fomorians (Fomoire) and their allies, it is the former who retain this special advantage (along with another less astonishing one):[1]

[1] Elizabeth A. Gray (ed.), *Cath Maige Tuired: The Second Battle of Mag Tuired* (Irish Texts Society, vol. LII, Naas, Ireland, 1982), pp. 55–57.

Now every day the battle was drawn up between the race of the Fomorians and the Túatha Dé Danann, but there were no kings or princes waging it, only fierce and arrogant men.

One thing which became evident to the Fomorians in the battle seemed remarkable to them. Their weapons, their spears and their swords, were blunted; and those of their men who were killed did not come back the next day (*ocus an romarbad dia feruib-sium ní ticdis íernabháruch*). That was not the case with the Túatha Dé Danann: although their weapons were blunted one day, they were restored the next because Goibniu the smith was in the smithy making swords and spears and javelins. He would make those weapons with three strokes. Then Luchtaine the carpenter would make the spearshafts in three chippings, and the third chipping was a finish and would set them in the socket of the spear. After the spearheads were in the side of the forge he would throw the sockets with the shafts, and it was not necessary to set them again. Then Crédne the brazier would make the rivets with three strokes, and he would throw the sockets of the spears at them, and it was not necessary to drill holes for them; and they stayed together this way.

Now this is what used to kindle the warriors who were wounded there so that they were more fiery the next day (*is edh dano doberiud bruth isna hógaib nogontais ann, comtarániu íarnauhárach*): Dían Cécht, his two sons Octriuil and Míach, and his daughter Airmed were chanting spells (*dícetul*) over the well named Sláine (*foran tibrait .i. Sláine a hainm*). They would cast their mortally-wounded men into it as they were struck down; and they were alive when they came out (*Focertdidis a n-athgoíte indte immairlestis; botar bí notégdis esde*). Their mortally-wounded men were healed through the power of the incantation made by the four physicians who were around the well (*bati[r] slán a n-athgoíte tre nert an dícetail na cethri lege robátar imon tibrait*).

Now that was damaging to the Fomoire, and they picked a man to reconnoitre the battle and the practices of the Túatha Dé—Rúadán, the son of Bres and of Bríg, the daughter of the Dagda—because he was a son and a grandson of the Túatha

Dé. Then he described to the Fomoire the work of the smith and the carpenter and the brazier and the four physicians who were around the well. They sent him back to kill one of the *áes dána,* Goibniu. He requested a spearpoint from him, its rivets from the brazier, and its shaft from the carpenter; and everything was given to him as he asked. Now there was a woman there grinding weapons, Crón the mother of Fíanlach; and she ground Rúadán's spear. So the spear was given to Rúadán by his maternal kin, and for that reason a weaver's beam is still called "the spear of the maternal kin" in Ireland.

But after the spear had been given to him, Rúadán turned and wounded Goibniu. He pulled out the spear and hurled it at Rúadán so that it went through him; and he died in his father's presence in the Fomorian assembly. Bríg came and keened for her son. At first she shrieked, in the end she wept. Then for the first time weeping and shrieking were heard in Ireland. (Now she is the Bríg who invented a whistle for signalling at night.)

Then Goibniu went into the well and he became whole (*Luid trá Gaibniu fon tibrait 7 ba slán-side*). The Fomoire had a warrior named Octríallach, the son of the Fomorian king Indech mac Dé Domnann. He suggested that every single man they had should bring a stone from the stones of the River Drowes to cast into the well Sláine in Achad Abla to the west of Mag Tuired, to the east of Lough Arrow. They went, and every man put a stone into the well. For that reason the cairn is called Octríallach's Cairn. But another name for that well is Loch Luibe, because Dían Cécht put into it every herb that grew in Ireland.

Among the Welsh, there may be a historical basis for the conflict that, in the story of Branwen in the second branch of the *Mabinogi,* sets the men of the Isle of the Mighty against the Gwyddyl of Iwerddon; in other words, the British of Great Britain against the Gaelic folk of Ireland. But most of the characters who direct the action, like Manawydan, are certainly historicized gods. The peace has just been broken through the malevolence of a Briton named Efnisien, and a bloody battle is immediately joined. It quickly becomes apparent that the Irish are making use of the great power:[2]

> The Irish began to kindle a fire beneath the cauldron of rebirth. Corpses were thrown into the cauldron until it was full (*ac yna y dechrewis y Gwydyl kynneu tan dan y peir dadeni, ac yna y byrywyt y kalaned yn y peir, yny uei yn llawn*), and the next morning they rose up fighting as well as before, except they could not speak (*ac y kyuodyn tranoeth y bore yn wyr ymlad kystal a chynt, eithyr na ellynt dywedut*). But when Efnisien saw the corpses, and no room at all for the men of the Isle of the Mighty, he thought, "Dear God, alas! that I have caused this desolation of men of the Isle of the Mighty! And shame on me unless I find a way to deliver them from this" (*a meuyl ymi, ony cheissaf i waret rac hynn*).
>
> He hid himself, then, among the Irish corpses, and two bare-bottomed Irish came and threw him into the cauldron as an Irishman. He stretched himself out in the cauldron, then, until the cauldron broke in four pieces, and his heart as well (*Emystynnu idaw ynteu yn y peir, yny dyrr y peir yn pedwar dryll, ac yny dyrr y galon ynteu*). From that came such victory as the men of the Isle of the Mighty got, and their only victory was the escape of seven men.

Seven very important "men," as a matter of fact, because among them, besides Manawydan, was Bran, the hero whose head, later buried as a talisman at the site of London, failed to stave off the Norman conquest, but has insured the United Kingdom against invasion from the continent ever since.

One of the versions of the Greek Gigantomachy (the Battle of the Giants) presents two elaborate forms of the same theme:

> Now the gods [reports Apollodorus[3]] had an oracle (λόγιον) that none of the giants could perish at the hand of gods, but that with the help of a mortal they would be made

[2] P. K. Ford (trans.), *The Mabinogi* (Berkeley and Los Angeles, 1977), pp. 69–70.

[3] *Library* 1.6.1 (trans. by J. G. Frazer, Cambridge, Mass., 1967).

an end of. Learning of this, Gē, the Earth, sought for a simple (φάρμακον) to prevent the giants from being destroyed even by a mortal. But Zeus forbade the Dawn and the Moon and the Sun to shine, and then, before anybody else could get it, he culled the simple himself (τὸ μὲν φάρμακον αὐτὸς ἔτεμε φθάσας), and by means of Athena summoned Hercules to his help. Hercules first shot Alcyoneus with an arrow, but when the giant fell on the ground he somewhat revived. However, at Athena's advice Hercules dragged him outside Pallene, and so the giant died.

Thus it comes as no surprise that in India the war of the gods and demons, with its innumerable shifts of fortune, also contains an episode of this sort: the demons have at their disposal a secret means for reviving the dead; the gods endeavor to learn this secret, and by means of a well-chosen emissary, one whom the chaplain of the demons cannot in decency turn away, they succeed. We do not know what form this secret actually takes, how this *vidyā saṁjīvanī*, this "science of reanimation" works in practice—whether it involves medicaments, physical intervention, or merely incantation. But the important thing is that this advantage does not belong directly to the race of the demons nor to any one of them. Rather, their possession of it is ensured by the kāvya whom they have engaged on their behalf. It is Kāvya Uśanas and he alone, at first, who owns and administers this secret.

When the son of the chaplain of the gods comes asking to be received as an apprentice under the chaplain of the demons and enrolls for a thousand years, we might suppose that Kāvya Uśanas understands from the beginning what he is after; the demons understand it perfectly. He nevertheless accepts the young man, and for five hundred years neither one of them brings up the issue that could have put them at odds. Would the master in the end have handed down to this exemplary student, after his thousand years of service, the secret that gave him his power? We do not know. But he finds himself suddenly in the predicament of either having to hand it over or lose his daughter whom he loves above everything else in the world. He passes it on. After all, he is not the real loser—at most he loses only his monopoly and thence becomes all the more indispensable to the demons, because in default of the advantage that they used to have but have no longer, he still ensures them parity with the gods. If he abandons them, it will be the ruin of them: the divine warriors will come back to life, but not theirs, and the first real crisis would mean their complete surrender.

2. KAŪS AND THE ELIXIR OF LIFE

For the Zoroastrians, the history of the world, past, present, and future, is an ongoing struggle between the good and evil elements of creation—an amplification of the pre-Zoroastrian, Indo-Iranian, and doubtless already Indo-European struggle between the gods and demons. In this struggle, life belongs to Ōhrmazd, death to Ahriman. The primordial man Gaya Marətan, "Mortal Life," his offspring Mašya and Mašyānag, "Mortal Man" with his sister and wife "Mortal Woman," and the abstracted entity Amərətāṯ, "Im-mortality" (non-death), suffice to show how much importance these two conflicting notions had in the reformed religion. But after the primordial times with their legendary figures it became impossible for a hero, however prestigious he might be, to intervene in the cosmic conflict, either for or against the good, by so powerful a means as the ability to resurrect the dead, undoing or even suspending the work of death: Amərətāṯ belongs to God, and God alone. Thus it is not in his conflicts with God nor in his ambiguous relationship with the dīvs that Kaūs activates, or conversely withholds, a power almost identical to that which Kāvya Uśanas exercises on behalf of the dānavas. Specifically, it is not in the assault that he mounted against heaven at the head of an army of demons (Christensen compared this with the Greek Gigantomachy, which in turn, as we have just recalled, harbors a variant of this theme). It happens, more humbly, in an episode that despite its charm is a secondary one, no element of which oversteps the boundaries of heroic society—the one that Herman Lommel identified in 1938.[4]

[4] Above, p. 22.

Firdausi's Rustam is a great and good hero, the model hero, but also, for a prince of questionable character like Kaūs, a hero at once invaluable for his bravery and unsettling because of his uprightness. More than once Rustam's extraordinary feats pull Kaūs out of the enormous dangers his own flightiness places him in. It is to Rustam that Kaūs owes his ultimate success in the ill-advised and difficult campaign in the Māzandarān. It is Rustam who delivers him from his captivity in Arabia, and Rustam again is among those who recover him after his wretched fall from the heaven he had wanted to conquer. But Rustam judges his master, judges harshly, and on occasion he speaks out. Kaūs for his part is resentful of this loyal power, on whom in the last resort his security depends. In short, their relationship, at least in the king's low-minded perception, is one of threatening rivalry.

Hardly had they made peace with each other after one of those outbursts when the tragic encounter of father and son took place—Rustam, the father, failing to recognize his son Sōhrab until he had fatally wounded him, at the end of a duel in which he himself barely escaped alive, because in this remarkable race of Sistanian heroes, the son is the equal of his father. For a long time Sōhrab lies dying:[5]

> Some time having passed in this manner, Rustam approached his son, his soul in torment. All the great ones, including Tūs, Gūdarz, and Kustaham, were with him. All those good men raised their voices in prayer to God on behalf of the noble Rustam, begging him to ease this suffering, to help Rustam to bear up under this anguish. Rustam seized a dagger, to separate his worthless head from his body. The great ones fell upon him, blood flowing from their eyelashes, and Gūdarz said to him, "What good will it do you now to send the world up in smoke? If you gave yourself a hundred wounds, what help would it be to your noble son? If he still has some time to live on the Earth, live he will, and you should live with him; and if this child must leave the world, keep in mind that nothing on earth lasts forever. Every one of us is

[5] *Le Livre des Rois* II: 174ff.

prey to Death, whether his head is adorned with a coronet or covered with a helmet. When the time comes, we have to die, and what will come after life, we do not know. Who then, O Sipāhdār, is exempt from the fear of death? Does not every man have to mourn for himself? Whether Death's road be long or short, we are all lost when we cross paths with him."

Then Rustam said to Gūdarz, "O mighty, brilliant-souled hero! Take a message from me to Kaūs. Tell him what evil has befallen me: 'With my dagger I have torn the heart of my brave son—curse my hand! If you remember what I have done for you, show this once that there is compassion in your heart for my distress. Send me some of that balm which is kept in your storehouse, the one that heals wounds, in all haste, with a cup of wine. Maybe, by your kind favor, Sōhrab will be healed, and become as I am, one of the servants who stand before your throne.' "

The General departed, swift as the wind, and carried the message to Kaūs. The king answered him, "Who in the world is more honored than Rustam? I have the greatest regard for him, and could wish no harm to come to him. But if I gave him my elixir, his son, with his elephant-sized body, would come back to life, and as Rustam's ally would make him more powerful—this would undoubtedly lead to my death. And if he should ever do harm to me, could I then punish him as he deserved? You have heard Rustam say, 'Who is Kaūs? And yet he is king—but who then is Tūs?' Who in the world could keep in check a man with such pride and strength, and such arms and legs? Would he remain humbly beneath my throne, would he march under my royal insignia, he who has abusively defied me, and dishonored me in front of my troops? If his son remains alive, my hand will be full of dust. Have you not heard Sōhrab's words? Are you not a great man who has seen the world? He would lop off the heads of a thousand Iranians, and hang Kaūs alive on the gallows. If he lives, great and small will cower before him. He who helps to rescue his enemy creates an evil reputation for himself in the world." Gūdarz listened to him and returned at once. He came to where Rustam was, flying like smoke, and told him, "The king's evil temper is like colocynth, that never ceases to bear

> bitter fruit. Because of his hard-heartedness he has not a friend in the world, and he will never sacrifice a thing to soften the pain of any man. Go to him yourself, and try to lighten his black soul."
>
> Rustam ordered his servants to prepare a sheet woven of gold, and to lay his son upon it with golden flowers, so that he could be brought to the king. The elephant-bodied hero started on his way. But someone ran after him with all speed to tell him that Sōhrab had left the wide world, and he now needed a coffin instead of a palace. The father leaped up, and heaved a long sigh, rubbing his eyelids and covering them with blood. He leaped from his horse as fast as the wind, took off his helmet, and covered his head with dust. The chiefs of the army cried out all together, weeping and lamenting.

Kaūs has the bad taste to preach a Senecan *consolatio ad Rustamum*, more vain than the vainest by Nero's teacher. Rustam, before taking his son's body away to the land of his ancestors, has the patience to hear him out, his self-control giving the lie to the king's fears and jealousy:

> When Kaūs was informed of Sōhrab's death, he went to Rustam with a retinue, and said to him, "From Mount Elburz to the reed-nourishing water, everything is carried along by the motion of heaven, so one must not become attached to things of the Earth. One dies sooner, another later, but in the end all cross to the other side. Let your soul and heart take comfort for the loss of this one who has died, and turn your ears to the words of the wise. Even if you pulled heaven down to the ground, or burned up the world, you would not bring this dead man back to life. Remember that his soul will live forever in the other world. From afar I have seen his chest and his arms, his height, and his club. Fate has led him here with his army, only to get his death at your hand. What will you do? What help is there? How long will you weep for him who is gone?"

From the point of view of Kaūs this episode is a peak in the struggle for power, in which he single-mindedly warps his relationship with the most faithful of his generals. Though he possesses the elixir that heals even mortal wounds (this detail emerges from the statements Firdausi attributes to him), he refuses to use it to benefit a young hero in whom he sees only a dangerous and intolerable ally for his imagined rival. Thus reduced to a personal rivalry, or a delusion of one, the theme loses in scope what it gains in pathos. As for our comparative study, what is important lies first in what Lommel had already discovered; namely, that despite his transformation into a king, Kaūs retains a trait better suited to a sorcerer —the possession of a drug that saves even the most seriously wounded from death (the *ante mortem* equivalent to resurrection); consequently, this trait must come to him from a prehistory in which his prototype, like the Indic Kāvya Uśanas, was a sorcerer. Second, this prerogative is mentioned only in the context of a request and a denial between two men, one of whom, the possessor, considers the other, the supplicant, his potential enemy, so that in his eyes the sharing of the drug would lead to a fatal shift in the balance of power.

Thus we can see how, starting with the probable Indo-Iranian form of the tradition (of which the Indian version is undoubtedly a more faithful representative), the ideological framework of Zoroastrianism and the growing interest of men of letters in the impulses and weaknesses of the soul, to the exclusion of more cosmic concerns and workings, has produced this episode that only Firdausi preserves, and charged the ambivalent Kaūs with yet another sin, one he moreover will not have to expiate.

3. KĀVYA UŚANAS, KAY ŪS AND THE MANIPULATION OF AGE

There are two ways of overcoming death: reviving those who have died in the prime of life or what amounts to the same thing, healing those who have received mortal wounds; and curing that implacable malady of growing old, whether by assuring to men the eternal youth that is the normal state of the gods or by dispelling old age after it has come and replacing it with its opposite. Kāvya

Uśanas had both of these powers in his magical arsenal. He revived dead warriors and his assassinated disciple, and also transformed old men into young. But his second power was used also and primarily in reverse—not as a favor but as a chastisement, punishing young offenders with instant senescence. In other words, the full definition of his power was that he manipulated at will, either by accelerating or by reversing it, the normal course of aging.

Such, from the standpoint of Kāvya Uśanas, is the sense of the third and final episode of his story; an episode that (still regarding Kāvya Uśanas) forms a diptych with the first. Throughout this long and varied chain of events, his supernatural power manifests itself in nothing but resurrections and reversals of aging. Here we need to be more specific. The curse with which he strikes Yayāti, particular though it be, would not have to come from a specialist in this type of manipulation: the punishments dished out by ṛṣis and others so endowed cover a wide range of metamorphoses, and it is no more difficult to make an old man young again than to change a human being into a serpent or a woman into a man. But Kāvya Uśanas is more intimately linked with the actual mechanism of the procedure. After cursing Yayāti, he not only offers in a general way to transfer to one of his sons (if Yayāti can find one to volunteer) the old age with which he has been struck; he also provides him with the technical formula for this transfer, and the recipe consists of "thinking of him," "being mindful of him"—Kāvya Uśanas; thus we must conclude that it is Kāvya Uśanas who directly intervenes and effects the swapping of ages.

A very similar power belonged also to the Iranian Kavi Usan, to judge from the Pahlavi and Persian texts. It is a solely benign power, and in the positive direction—the rejuvenation of the aged, at no cost. The texts present this in a variety of ways, but always in connection with the marvelous and sumptuous edifices the king had had built for himself, generally by the enslaved demons.

According to *Dēnkart* 9.22.4,[6] a summary of the *Sūtkar Nask*, the seven castles, one of gold, two of silver, two of steel, and two

[6] Above, p. 46.

of crystal, which he had had raised on Mount Elburz, had a magic quality: "Every man enfeebled by old age, whose soul was attuned to bodily suffering, upon reaching this place and going quickly all about it had his age fade away and his strength and youth return to him—orders were given not to turn men away from this gate—and he would present the appearance of a youth of fifteen."[7]

The *Greater Bundahišn*, after having mentioned the five palaces, one of gold, two of crystal, and two of steel, adds:[8] "therefrom issued all tastes, and waters of the springs giving immortality, which smite old age—that is, when a decrepit man enters by this gate, he comes out as a youth of fifteen years from the other gate—and also dispel death."

The Islamic authors, who readily describe these palaces, have not in general mentioned this feature. As Christensen remarks,[9] however, "a last remnant of this almost forgotten motif is found in a remark in the book of Bīrūnī about India, where we read that Kay Ūs, as a decrepit old man, betook himself to Mount Qāf [substituted for Mount Elburz?], and came back transformed into a handsome and strong youth, having made himself a chariot out of the clouds." The theme is altered here in the sense that Kay Ūs himself is the beneficiary of the treatment, and only he; but the text discloses that he was also the effectuator: he knew what he was going to do, and what he would gain on the mountain. Generalized more broadly as "immortality," it is doubtless the same theme that gave rise to mentions like that in the Middle Persian commentary on *Vidēvdāt* 2,[10] or that in *Mēnōk-i-Xrat* 8.27–28, according to which Yim and Kay Ūs (and in the latter text Frētōn) were created

[7] Madan, p. 815, line 22–p. 816, line 5: *martōm kē zōr hac zarmān tarvēnītak ut ǰān nazdīh ō pazdakīh i hac tan būt, ō hān i ōy mān āyāft, tēǰ pēramōn hān mān vāzēnīt, zarmān haciš ōsānīhist ut zōr ut ǰuvānīh apāc mat (ē framōš dāt ēstēt ku martōmān pat dar apāc mā dārēt); 15 sālak handēmān būt.*

[8] Anklesaria, pp. 270–271, slightly emended by Fr. de Menasce; the end reads: *kad zarmān mart pat ēn darak andar šavēt, apurnāy i 15 sāl pat ēn darak bērōn āyēt, ut marg-ič bē zanēt.*

[9] *Les Kayanides*, p. 109.

[10] James Darmesteter, *The Zend Avesta* 3 (Westport, Conn., 1972): 26.

immortal and became mortal through their own fault; it was for having tried to conquer heaven that Kay Ūs lost this precious gift, according to *Dēnkart* 9.22.12.[11]

The texts we cited first, which attribute to Kay Ūs, through his magical palaces, the general power of rejuvenation for the benefit of all men, are the most precise, and for us the most interesting. These texts render it likely that the Indo-Iranian prototype already contained, besides the power to save from imminent or effective death, this mastery of the aging process, which the Indic and Iranian derivatives present in two different forms.

[11] *Les Kayanides*, p. 79.

V

TWO TALES

1. THE LEGEND OF KĀVYA UŚANAS AND THE TYPE OF KAVI USAN

Thus the character traits and the actions, as well as the social status transposed into the invisible world, which the tale in the first book of the *Mahābhārata* attributes to Kāvya Uśanas, find precise accordances in the Iranian Kavi Usan. These matching traits can be ascribed no doubt in a form more resembling the Indic than the Iranian version, to the Indo-Iranian figure whose name they both inherit. But the Indic story is no disorganized collection of character traits and actions; it is truly a tale, and very tightly constructed. In its context in the poem, the main characters are neither Kāvya Uśanas himself nor the demons who are at war with the gods, nor Kaca, nor even the pair of treacherous friends Devayānī and Śarmiṣṭhā—everything is centered on Yayāti; the whole story is intended to explain why Yayāti's heir, contrary to the rule, is the youngest of his five sons, Pūru, the ancestor and eponym of the heroes of the poem.[1] It is useful and simple to spell this out, particularly as there is no reason not to call it an intentional plan.

Each of the first two episodes provides at its end one of the two conditions of the adultery that will provoke, in the third, the

[1] Cf. above, pp. 39–40, and *The Destiny of a King*, chapter 1.

premature aging of the guilty king and the self-sacrifice and the reward of his youngest son. These two elements are, first, the fate that Kaca imposes on Devayānī, that she will not marry a brahmin (perhaps, more anciently, a kaví); second, the demand that Devayānī makes on the demons to surrender to her their princess Śarmiṣṭhā as a slave who will accompany her as such to the house of her husband, whoever he may be. Everything else follows from this: no longer able to hope for a brahmin husband, Devayānī demands to be married to the kṣatriya who took her hand in order to pull her from the well, namely King Yayāti. Then she takes her slave-princess to the house of her husband, from whom the woman discreetly solicits and receives sexual attention and motherhood; when the deceit is discovered, Yayāti is cursed by his father-in-law, and so on.

But these first two episodes, convergent as they are, are already linked together by a tie of causality: if, in the first, Kāvya Uśanas had not shared with Kaca the formula for reviving the dead, the demons would have more freedom in their dealings with him, as they could consider coolly the possibility of allowing him to leave, assuming that he would at least not enter the service of their enemies. But since the gods are now, thanks to Kaca, in possession of the formula, keeping Kāvya Uśanas in their camp is a matter of life and death. Thus they agree to all the conditions, including the one that makes their princess the slave of their chaplain's daughter—particularly humiliating for the king, and which in the last resort will rebound against Devayānī.

Within each episode the causality is no less strict. To consider only the first, it is natural for the gods to send the son of their priest to the holder of the great secret—Kāvya Uśanas would receive no one but the son of a colleague. It is believable for the daughter of Kāvya Uśanas, who can get her father to do anything, to be receptive to the attentions of this handsome young man, and just as natural for the demons to want at all costs to liquidate this sort of spy. When they see how Kāvya Uśanas resuscitates him by calling him out from the bellies of the wolves, it is ingenious but natural for the demons to dispatch him, in a bumper of ash-laced punch, into the belly of the reviver—how were they to know that Kāvya Uśanas would kill himself in order to rescue his disciple? At this point two possibilities are open to Kāvya Uśanas: either to forgo calling forth Kaca from his belly, or to impart the great secret to him before making him its beneficiary in hopes of being repaid in kind. As the predictable insistence of Devayānī, which takes the form of extortion by threat of suicide, precludes the first solution, Kāvya Uśanas resolves to run the risks of the second, and he is not disappointed; once restored to life, Kaca revives him. If it is reasonable that five hundred years after this, his term expired, Kaca wants to return to the gods with the hard-won secret, it is no less natural that the smitten and spoiled Devayānī makes claim to be paid for her services and demands marriage. But marriage proves doubly impossible: one does not marry the daughter of one's guru, and above all, having lived several hours in the bowels of Kāvya Uśanas and having escaped only by a kind of caesarean operation, Kaca has literally become his son in the flesh—his guru, he says, has become both his father and his mother—and for him to marry Devayānī would be to commit incest. Consequently, with our knowledge of this girl's character, we are not surprised to see her choose her revenge to hurt the ingrate: she tries to nullify with a curse all the profit that Kaca has gained from a thousand years of effort. After this, how could Kaca not attack this prideful woman's weakest point, by condemning her to become déclassée the day she is married?

There is no use prolonging this commentary; the reader can readily verify that everything is equally well organized in the second and third episodes. If by chance one of the elements in the series of causes and effects seems to be lacking in precision or inevitability, he will take care not to judge according to our habitual ways of thinking. Personally, I have found only one point, a very important one, which might at first appear weak, but it is not: the dilemma in which Kāvya Uśanas finds himself caught and from which he gets out only by communicating the secret of resurrection. "Either," he says, "Kaca must remain dead, in the form of ashes, trapped in my belly as he is now—in which case I lose my daughter, driven to despair; or else I must call him out and have him pierce my side as he did those of the wolves, and kill me in doing so." The Western reader has a mind to speak up here, to suggest a third way, natural if malodorous: let Kāvya wait patiently for a day or two, or let him use a potion to speed up the normal process of digestion. When the ashes have been evacuated along with the feces, he can resuscitate Kaca while extricating him from that disagreeable matrix, requiring no further measures. But this is impossible: a story in the *Mahābhārata* in which a very similar motif appears proves that once digested an absorbed being can no longer be brought back to life.[2] In the third book, the great wise man Lomaśa recounts to Yudhiṣṭhira, near the watering hole of another great sage, Agastya, the story of Vātāpi:

The demon Ilvala, sworn enemy of the brahmins, has decided to exterminate their race, and he resorts to a simple method. He invites his intended victims, one by one or in small groups, to a good meal and serves to them in a stew his brother, the demon Vātāpi, transformed beforehand into a goat, killed, and cooked. As soon as the plates are empty, he calls Vātāpi by his name, and the latter springs forth intact, piercing the sides of the guests, who naturally do not survive. Ilvala has already seriously thinned the ranks of brahmins on earth when a twist in the plot, very interesting although not important here, brings to his house the wise Agastya, the super-brahmin, in the company of three kings. Ilvala welcomes him, changes Vātāpi into a goat and prepares the dish. The three kings are terrified. Agastya reassures them: "Do not worry," he says, "I will eat the great Asura on my own." Sure enough, in the course of the banquet Agastya eats the entire goat, to the greatest pleasure of the host, whose grudge is only against brahmins. When after the meal Ilvala calls his brother in a loud voice, nothing happens, except that Agastya gives out with a prodigious fart as resounding as a thunderclap. "Come out, Vātāpi!" Ilvala cries out several more times. Agastya then explains to him, laughing, "How

[2] *Mahābhārata* III, 94–97 (van Buitenen, 2: 411–415).

can the Asura come out, now that I have digested him?" An easy feat for a sage of Agastya's class, the miracle consisted in granting himself instantaneous digestion, which was completed before Ilvala had time to execute his usual gambit. But one can see that, accelerated or not, complete digestion leaves the resurrective technique, which closely resembles that of Kāvya Uśanas, with nothing to work on. The story of Vātāpi thus establishes that the dilemma in which Kāvya suddenly found himself caught was compelling, and moreover that he had to decide quickly, before digestion set in. Of course one could object that the ashes, being unassimilable, would have been eliminated intact in any case, within the relatively short time that is familiar to us; this would be asking a lot of the narrator's physiological knowledge.

Corresponding to this meticulously constructed tale, Iran presents not a superimposable story, but simply—illustrated or made use of in distinct narrative fragments composed in different periods—a homologous character, a parallel state of affairs between God and the demons, analogous wealth, a similar recipe allowing the healing (or nonhealing) of a fatal wound, and another enabling the transformation of old men into young. What we recover for Indo-Iranian prehistory, then, is a type for the mythical kaví, not his history.

2. OTHER TRADITIONS ABOUT KĀVYA UŚANAS

But even in India, the long coherent text of the first book of the *Mahābhārata* does not exhaust what the authors of the epic knew of Kāvya Uśanas, and it happens that this further information, far removed from what we have just studied or giving only distant variants of it, also matches elements in the Iranian dossier.

The most important account is found in one of the two encyclopedic books, accretions of multiple eras, in which Bhīṣma, slain in delayed fashion on the edge of the battlefield of Kurukṣetra, overloads Yudhiṣṭhira and a few others with the wonders and the dross of his knowledge of all sorts of things. Like many of these teachings, this one is imparted in a frame, with a śivaistic tinge: long gone is the happy time when the chaplain of the demons could hold in check the power of an eminent but ordinary god like Indra; it is a greater divinity, Śiva, that he is going to meet in his ventures.[3] The poet begins with an enticing series of questions by Yudhiṣṭhira which, as is frequent in this part of the poem, Bhīṣma does not fully answer:

> What led the celestial ṛṣi, the magnanimous Uśanas, also called *kavi,* to take sides with the demons and oppose the gods? Why did he want to diminish the strength of the gods? Why have the demons always been at war against the most eminent of the gods? For what reason was Uśanas, endowed with the splendor of the immortals, given the name Śukra? How did he attain this degree of excellence? Why, in spite of possessing such great élan, did he not succeed in going all the way to the center of the firmament?

The answer to the first question is given only by an allusion to a "just grievance" that the kaví would have had against the gods, one that is clarified by the authorized commentary: at Indra's request, the mother of Uśanas had been decapitated by Viṣṇu. Though the *Mahābhārata* makes no mention elsewhere of this legend, the *Vāyu-Purāṇa* expands on it, but in such a way that it no longer explains what it ought to have explained.[4] There, in fact, Uśanas had already previously agreed to enlist in the service of the demons, and the murder of his mother is the consequence, not the cause, of that pledge. During the absence of Uśanas, who had gone to ask Mahādeva-Śiva for the prayer that would ensure their success, the demons, left to themselves and frightened by the gods, appealed to their priest's mother, the wife of Bhṛgu, Divyā. Taking her role seriously, she undertook to deprive Indra of his station and to set fire to the world of the gods. At the request of Indra, who moreover entered into his body, Viṣṇu killed her, and as a

[3] *Mahābhārata* XII (Calc. śl. 10669–10696).

[4] A detailed summary of the narrative (sections 97–98) and of parallel texts is to be found in V. R. Ramachandra Dikshitar, *The Purāṇa Index* I (1950): 370, s.v. "Kāvya."

result, before resuscitating his wife, Bhṛgu condemned the great god by a curse to be born seven times in human form. But let us go back to the twelfth book of the *Mahābhārata*. We read there the following, which answers Yudhiṣṭhira's other questions well: Through the power of his *yoga*, Uśanas entered the body of the god Kubera, the keeper of Indra's treasury. Depriving him of his freedom in the manner of the devils who become lodged in possessed persons, he robbed him of all his riches, then carried them off when he left his body. Kubera complained to Maheśvara-Śiva, who was very angry and decided to do away with the culprit. He waylaid him, his spear in front of him, ready to strike. Again by the force of his yoga, Uśanas attached himself to the only point that the lance was unable to reach: the very point of the weapon. But Śiva bent his spear, caught him in his hand, and swallowed him. Uśanas then began wandering within the august entrails. Śiva devoted himself to great austerities, but soon—after a few million years—it became apparent that, far from exterminating him, the penance had made the parasite thrive and grow. Śiva reimmersed himself in yoga, closing all his natural openings. Uśanas for his part, while all the while singing the praises of the god who hosted him, resumed his roamings, with such success that Śiva returned to his first plan. "Leave by my urethra!" he cried, in order to be certain to see the culprit immediately upon his exit. Uśanas, who had no doubt expected to get out by the back route, had trouble finding this orifice and roamed in vain for some time, "burning with the force of Mahādeva." In the end he got out, and this is where he got his name of Śukra, "urine." It is also owing to this last clumsiness that he did not succeed (Śukra this time in the sense of "the planet Venus") in reaching the center of the firmament. Once outside, Uśanas found himself once again exposed to the spear of Śiva, but Śiva's wife, the goddess Umā, intervened, becoming by this action the mother of the escapee[5] and at the same time giving him a

[5] Śl. 10692: *putratvam agamad devyāḥ*

father: "This one who has become my son must not be killed by you, for whoever has come out of the belly of a god does not deserve death!" she said.[6] Śiva smiled and let Uśanas go.

This little saga recalls the competitions of shamans in the literatures of northern Asia, and such is indeed the normal color of these śivaistic stories. But we recognize here too, used in a different way, several important features of this character. First, having robbed the god of riches, Uśanas himself has become fabulously wealthy and, as is said in the third book of the epic, master of the treasures of the universe. Then, Uśanas and Śiva playing this time respectively the roles of Kaca and Uśanas in the first book (i.e., with Uśanas being the prisoner and not the prison), the scene that unfolds in Śiva's innards is patently inspired by the other, and ends in the same state of affairs. Whether he leaves by bursting forth or by urination, the being who has lived in the other's belly has become his son, and this intestinal paternity has the same moral and legal weight as ordinary procreation: Śiva can no longer kill Uśanas, and it would be incest for Kaca to marry the daughter of Uśanas. It is noteworthy too that, although in a different way and at a different stage in the process, it is a woman, Śiva's wife, who saves Uśanas, just as it is the daughter of Uśanas who saves Kaca.

We also recall how the Iranian Kay Ūs had ambitiously taken it into his head to take over heaven, how God let him advance with his troops to a certain point, then "when he had passed the clouds," flung him back to the earth, where, according to one text, he found he had lost his natural immortality: "Although he had entered the celestial world," says *Aogəmadaēča* 60, "he could not escape the dominion of death." And Bhīṣma teaches Yudhiṣṭhira that as a result of his passage through Śiva's urethra, Śukra—to be interpreted here, as I have pointed out, as the planet Venus—"did not succeed in reaching the center of the firmament." Perhaps these are two divergent applications of a single thought pattern, already

[6] Śl. 10693: *hiṃsanīyas tvayā naiva mama putratvam āgataḥ / na hi devodarāt kiścit niḥsṛto nāśam arhati*

Indo-Iranian and perhaps already astronomical or in any case cosmological, in form, with the area covered by the unsuccessful assault on the sky assimilated to the limited field of appearance of Venus.

The Purāṇic texts, as we have just seen in the *Vāyu-Purāṇa,* give certain other indications of the behavior and the exploits of Uśanas. Nearly always it has to do with episodes in the war between the gods and the demons, interpreted to the greatest glory of the savior—sometimes Viṣṇu, sometimes Śiva. Most of these episodes are either variations or proliferations of traditions already known. Thus, still following the *Vāyu-Purāṇa,* we have seen that Uśanas leaves the demons alone, exposed to the attacks of the gods, while he goeṣ to ask Śiva for the mantra, the formula that will give them victory: undoubtedly this formula is a watered-down form of the resuscitative knowledge that in the first book was to assure the victory of the demons. There is also mention elsewhere of a brief absence—ten years—on the part of the demons' priest,[7] but this was in order to live incognito with a young girl, the daughter of Indra. Bṛhaspati, the chaplain of the gods, took advantage of the occasion; he appeared to the demons in the guise of Uśanas and pretended to bring them the mantra of victory that he said he had learned; they accepted, he settled down among them, and this was not good for them. After ten years the real Uśanas returned, so that the demons saw before them two identical beings. They chose the wrong one and refused to believe the true Uśanas, who withdrew, offended. The demons soon realized their error. Moved with sympathy, he went to plead their case before Brahmā, who declared that several million years later they would recover their power. Indeed, under two disciples of Uśanas, Saṇḍa and Marka, the demons brought the gods to such a wretched state that Viṣṇu decided to take on bodily form; this is the cause of his human incarnations. There is apparently nothing in these stories of sorcerers useful to the comparativist.

Other features are more interesting, such as the following one,

[7] Dikshitar, *The Purāṇa Index.*

remarkable for its trifunctional character: in recompense for prodigious penances, Kāvya Uśanas was given three privileges by Mahādeva-Śiva: he would never be conquered, he would have wealth at his command, and he would enjoy immortality.[8] One will recall the Iranian tradition of the palaces made of precious materials in which Kay Ūs both displayed his riches and asserted his mastery of the three functions, lodging his cows in one, his horses or his armies in others, sometimes his priest in yet another, and reserving for himself the most sumptuous; the fountains of these palaces, among other privileges, gave immortality, the immortality that other texts ascribe directly to Kay Ūs, at least until his demented assault on heaven.

These accordances are valuable, but all they do is add a bit in bulk to the collection of features, and especially privileges, which are common to Kāvya Uśanas and Kay Ūs; they do not, any more than the tale in the first book of the *Mahābhārata*, allow us to glimpse a prototype in which these features were already dynamically and harmoniously employed in a unified plot. We have not even tried to compare this tale from the first book with the "story of Kay Ūs" which occurs with slight variations in most of the texts of the Islamic period, in particular Firdausi and al-Thaʿālibī, and of which *Greater Bundahišn* 33.8–10 already gives a summary. This guarantees that it was already established in the famous *Xvatāy Nāmak*, now lost along with its early adaptations, which seems to have been the main source of all this epic literature, of all these late attestations of the "national tradition."[9] If I do not analyze this story here, it is because it is much less tightly constructed than the Indic tale, and also because I have myself compared the two without being able to observe any parallels in the articulation of the episodes.

[8] Ibid.

[9] Christensen, *Les Kayanides*, pp. 40–41; Wikander, "Sur le fonds commun indo-iranien des épopées de la Perse et de l'Inde" (see above, p. 8, n. 17), pp. 313–315 (and 313, n. 4). The word "national," as opposed to "priestly," is an unfortunate choice, but it has become a *terminus technicus* here.

VI

MASTERS AND DISCIPLES, MEN AND WOMEN

1. THE DISCIPLE IN THE BODY OF THE MASTER, THE GRANDSON IN THE BODY OF THE GRANDFATHER

The list of fragmentary correspondences is not yet complete. There are a few more that are difficult to evaluate and even to define, but which when supported by the foregoing at least merit some thought. Here are two examples.

We have just seen how the episode of Kaca held captive in the entrails of his master had caught the imagination of the Indian poets so that they produced, recast to the disadvantage of Kāvya Uśanas and amplified to the scale of the "great god," a śivaistic variant. It may be too that the episode was more essential than it appears at first sight to the character and the role of the kaví. In any case, the Middle Persian and epic tradition reports something different, but in the same vein, about Kay Ūs (Kaūs).

When this king had tried to scale the heavens (says *Dēnkart* 9.22.7–12,[1] summarizing the *Sūtkar Nask*) the punishment was multiple: the Glory of the Kavis abandoned him; Kaūs fell to the earth and took refuge in Lake Vourukaša; and as a more immediate threat, the usual messenger of God, Nēryōsang, pursued him

[1] Madan, p. 816, line 11–p. 817, line 10.

in order to kill him. But following on his heels, the *fravaši* of his future grandson, Kay Xusrōy—his son's son—protected him. To Nēryōsang, who tried to push her aside, the fravaši cried out, identifying herself with the one for whom she was in advance both soul and guardian angel:

> Do not kill him, O Nēryōsang, furtherer of the world! For if you kill this man, O Nēryōsang, mover of the world, a champion destroyer of Tūrān will not be born, because from this man [Kaūs] will be begotten a man by the name of Siyāvaxš, and from Siyāvaxš I will be begotten, I who am Xusrōy, I who will draw out the one who is the most heroic (*vīrtom*) from Tūrān [i.e., Frāsiyāp], he who destroys many troops and armies. . . . It is I who, reversing the luck of battle, will crush his troops and armies, I who will drive off into the distance the king of Tūrān.

These words impressed Nēryōsang. He decided not to kill Kaūs, whose only penalty was thus that he became mortal.[2]

Frāsiyāp (Avestan Fraŋrasyan) is the great legendary chief whose wars against several of the Kayanids and already against Manuščihr symbolize, in the historical interpretation, the ongoing conflict between Iran and Tūrān, and it is indeed at the hands of Kay Xusrōy (Husrav), the first "Khosroës," that his rule and his life will come to an end. This trait of proleptic salvation through a grandson is not unknown in the epic of the Islamic period, but there Xusrōy's fravaši and the moving scene that it inspires disappear, replaced by a simple remark by God: "Kay Kaūs fell miserably and vanished," says al-Thaʿālibī,[3] "but God did not wish him to perish, because he knew and had decreed that from Kay Kaūs

[2] Christensen, *Les Kayanides*, pp. 78–79, whose translation has been considerably improved by Fr. de Menasce. On p. 82, Christensen arbitrarily rejects this episode: "The account of the intervention of the fravaši of Kay Xusrav, who saves Kay Ūs from the hands of Nēryōsang, is a typical product of the imagination of the mobads." Actually, the doctrine of the fravašis merely reoriented in a Zoroastrian direction the traditional scene intended to explain the dynastic solidarity of the grandfather and of the grandson he carries within him.

[3] *Histoire des Rois des Perses*, p. 167.

would be born Siyāvūš, and from Siyāvūš, Kay Khosroa, who was destined to put Afrāsyāb to death."

Unlike the ambiguous, mercurial Kay Ūs, whose relationship with God oscillates between obedience and revolt, Kay Xusrōy, the son of his ill-fated son, will be entirely "good," and not only for God, but for Iran as well. Where the political indiscretions and religious instability of Kay Ūs have several times led the empire into great difficulties, Kay Xusrōy will rid it once and for all of its persistent enemy. But the episode of Nēryōsang and the fravaši points up, between these two dissimilar beings, a unity that is the very foundation of the notion of dynasty: Kay Ūs must survive, despite his revolt against God, in order for the useful and pious Kay Xusrōy to come into the world; and conversely, for the present Kay Ūs to escape punishment, the prefigurement (or the fravaši, or the voice) of his future grandson has to intercede. They are indissolubly bound by physiology, one genetically containing the other in his body and each saving the other.

We began to see earlier how the kavi-king of Iran could develop out of the kaví-magician of Indo-Iranian times, still clear and original in the *ṚgVeda* and preserved in the Indic epic as a specific variety of the brahmin type. Now we can see further: the Iranian kavis form a dynasty, embodied in the continuity of generations, the patrimony from father to son; the Indic and undoubtedly already Indo-Iranian kavís form a brotherhood, whose members are interdependent and in which knowledge is handed down from master to disciple. For the true kingship to be maintained in Iran, for the "Glory of the Kayanids" to continue its course from head to head, it must be transferred correctly, each link of the genealogy being in its turn as important as the rest. Likewise, in the guild of magicians, for the *vidyā*, the kāvya (the supernatural knowledge that is its common possession and its justification), to continue, the student is no less important than the master, and each needs the other. The epithet of Uśanas, Kāvya, "son of kaví," testifies perhaps to a state of affairs in which the disciple was often the son and the guild was already tending toward a dynasty. It is in this perspective that the episode of Kaca speaking from inside Kāvya

Uśanas takes on its full significance: the young Kaca is allied with the gods and Kāvya Uśanas with the demons, but in this form of the Indic ideology, the difference in loyalties is of little importance, and entails no moral note—Kaca gets no credit from the fact that he serves the gods, and the opposite choice that Kāvya Uśanas has made is not a transgression. The morality rests elsewhere, in the bosom of the guild (recast in the *Mahābhārata* as the brahmin class) to which they both belong. Once we have recognized this divergence between the systems of coordinates, the scene is close to the one in which the fravaši lends her voice to Kay Xusrōy, contained *in ovo* within Kay Ūs. Otherwise formulated, it is a question once again of "reciprocal salvation": if Kāvya Uśanas had not agreed to die while resuscitating his student, in the hope and confidence that his disciple would revive him in turn, it would be all over for Kaca, and if the disciple had not been true to his duty and had not revived his master, it would be the end of Uśanas; in either case the brotherhood would suffer grave damage.

Thus it may be that, in varying forms, we have to do on both sides with a scene conceived in very early times to give concrete expression to the solidarity of the senior and junior partners within a confraternity of magicians, and then, by the evolution of the latter, within a dynasty.

2. FORBIDDEN LOVES AND WOMEN'S REVENGE

The second parallelism concerns the role of the female—the daughter in the story of Kāvya Uśanas and the wife in that of Kay Ūs.

It will certainly have been noted that the formidable and intractable Kāvya Uśanas is, in every episode, under the thumb of his daughter Devayānī, who regularly either sways him to do what he had no mind to do (as in the last and dangerous resurrecting of Kaca), or stirs up his anger so that he will put his powers to use for her own vengeance (as in the enslavement of the daughter of the king of the demons and the sudden aging of Yayāti). This weakness is recognized by the gods, who, when they send Kaca to him as a student, advise the young man to ingratiate himself with the father, but especially with the daughter. Devayānī's power over her father is only one manifestation of her overbearing spirit. The first episode of the novel, which we analyzed regarding Kāvya Uśanas, is actually the close combination of two subjects: the unclouded relationship between student and teacher, plus the affair, evolving from smooth sailing to tempestuous, between the disciple and the master's daughter. By his attentions as much as by his qualities, Kaca has no trouble gaining Devayānī's favor, and it is on the double (or triple) urging of Devayānī that he is brought back from death and, finally, given possession of the secret which he came to seek for the gods. Things go sour later, when he wants to take his leave; Devayānī declares her love, and invoking the gratitude that he owes her, tries to force him into a union which would be doubly culpable: one does not marry the daughter of one's spiritual master, who is like a sister; still less does one marry the true sister who is the daughter of the man in whose entrails a peculiar (and happily rare) circumstance has placed one, and who has thus become at the same time one's father, because he is a man, and one's mother, because he carried one within himself. Kaca does not give in, Devayānī does not give up, and there is an exchange of curses, in which Devayānī takes the initiative: the secret that Kaca has so laboriously acquired will be useless in his hands. Kaca consoles himself by saying that he will pass it on to others. Thus, through the fault of his master's daughter and the incestuous love that she declares for him in vain, Kaca will have been only a middleman between his master and those he will inform, himself barred from using the magical power that his knowledge would have conferred.

The story of Kay Ūs contains a long and important episode whose analogy with this one is clearly seen if one recalls that what is in India a guild has become in Iran a dynasty, and that the relationship of father to son has been substituted for that of master to disciple. From a first union, Kay Ūs has a son, endowed with all the virtues, named in Middle Iranian Siyāvaxš, in Persian Siyāvūš.

A young woman, whom the king brought back from Arabia because she saved him from starving during his captivity and whom he married, sees the youth as soon as she arrives in the palace, and from that meeting on, the story falls into a well-known romantic mold. "What happened to Sudābeh," writes al-Thaᶜālibī,[4] "when she saw Siyāvūš from a distance was the same thing that happened to the wife of the governor of Egypt with the virtuous Joseph: she fell hopelessly in love with him; the earth, vast as it was, cramped her, her will was destroyed, and her passion for Siyāvūš reached its utmost limits."

There follows an account that in the best narrations contains a great deal of Choderlos de Laclos and a little of the Marquis de Sade, and whose detail is of little importance here.[5] Making use of her power over his father, the queen arranges, against the wishes of the son, for the women's quarters to be opened to him. Obediently, he goes in once, twice, but he resists the most demanding overtures and the best-contrived temptations. Then follows the vengeance of the queen, the slanderous accusation, even the somber staging of an abortion, which Siyāvūš escapes by the honest miracle of an ordeal. But he has had enough. He asks for and receives from his father an army command on the Turanian war front which will soon lead to his voluntary exile in the home of his enemy, who will welcome him at first and even give him his daughter in marriage, but who eventually will have him killed without his having ruled. Nevertheless, he will have begotten a son who, returning to his homeland, will succeed his paternal grandfather, avenge his father on his maternal grandfather, and once and for all defeat the Turanians: this will be Kay Xusraw. Thus, through the fault of his father's wife and the incestuous love that she declares for him in vain, Siyāvūš will have been only an intermediary between his father and his son, personally barred from the royal power that his patrimony should have assured him.

[4] Ibid., p. 171.
[5] Ibid., pp. 171–172.

Did the model of Potiphar's wife only formalize, only direct a more ancient account into a more familiar channel? Or, in order to elaborate the subject matter, have the authors drawn indiscriminately, directly or indirectly, from the Bible or from biblical folklore? The *Bundahišn*, summing up the story, already says that Kay Siyāvaxš led the army against the Turanian Frāsiyāp, but that "because of Sūtāvēh, the wife of (his father) Kay Ūs, Siyāvaxš did not return to Iran."[6] More anciently, besides the general list of kavis given in two Yašts that contains no details (and it is neither certain nor probable that all the persons named there are thought to have reigned), all that the surviving portions of the *Avesta* say about Kavi Syāvaršan, the father of Kavi Haosravah, is limited to the fact that he was killed by the Turanian Fraŋrasyan—which also does not imply that this kavi had been king. In any case, between Kavi Usaδan and Kavi Haosravah, about whom (especially the latter) the Yašts give some information, Kavi Syāvaršan is notable only for his death, and those who are named between Kavi Usaδan and him are not dwelt upon at all. One is therefore led to think that the nullification of kingship which affects the son of Kay Kaūs because of the latter's wife continues an ancient and important feature of the legend of Kavi Usaδan. If we take this tack, the analogous nullification of power which strikes the disciple of Kāvya Uśanas because of his daughter forces the age of this feature back even further, to Indo-Iranian times, and undoubtedly, like everything that appears in this set of correspondences, in a form closer to that of the *Mahābhārata* than to that of the *Shāh Nāmeh*. But in that case, what is the meaning of this power of a woman, daughter or spouse, over the great kaví, and of the disastrous effect of her intervention on the normal relationship between master and disciple (between royal father and crown prince, in the Iranian version)? At this point, where any objective grasp eludes one, one can, without committing oneself, form various hypotheses, notably the following.

[6] 33.10 (Anklesaria, p. 275); Christensen, *Les Kayanides*, p. 62.

In the society of the kaví magicians, as among the Gypsies of our time, women would have held a more important and more active position than was accorded them in normal priestly circles (brāhmaṇī, flāminica, etc.). In their relationships with a kaví, his employers therefore had to pay heed to his wife, his daughter, or his mother. This would also explain the role of the mother of Kāvya Uśanas in the Purāṇic literature: her son's employers, during an extended absence on his part, turn to his mother who actually takes charge. A distant support for this hypothesis perhaps is offered by the only society, Indo-European at least in part, where the same title appears, the Lydians.[7] Although in the inscriptions in the Lydian language, *kave-* can be a priest as well as a priestess (once "kave of Bakkhos and of Armas"; but once "kave of Demeter"; the other kaves are without qualification), it is solely as a title of a priestess of Artemis that the word is found in the accusative καυειν, in four attestations of a common Greek formula: ὁ δῆμος ἐτείμησεν Μελετίνην Θεογένους καυειν ἱερατεύσασαν ἀξίως τῆς θεοῦ, "the people honored Meletine, daughter of Theogenes, kave-, because she worthily exercised the function of priestess of the goddess."

But this peculiar power of women would have had its reverse side, at least in the "folklore of the brotherhood," in all the ways in which the cautionary tales of any society emphasize the dangers inherent in a government of women, or influenced by women, or affording great freedom to women.

[7] Olivier Masson, "Lydien *kaveś* (καύης)," *Jahrbuch für kleinasiatische Forschung* I (1950): 182–188; Roberto Gusmani, *Lydisches Wörterbuch* (Heidelberg, 1964), p. 150, s.v. "kave-"; cf. p. 278. In Latin and in Greek, the derivatives of the same root (that of *caveo*, κοέω) have tended toward legal meanings: Lat. *cautor*, "guarantor," also *causa*, "alleged motive, trial," etc; Gr. κοῖον, "pledge." But even in Greek, Hesychius gives the word κοίης (κόης), "priest of the Kabeiroi, who purifies a murderer." See Pierre Chantraine, *Dictionnaire étymologique de la langue grecque* II (Paris, 1970), s.v. κοέω and κοῖον.

[1982] The Lydian term *kavi* is probably an Iranian loanword, a fact that is problematic in view of the difference in usage, but which restricts the range of the Kāvya Uśanas ~ Kavi Usan correspondence to the Indo-Iranian domain.

First of all, as everyone knows, they lack judgment. Thus in the Purāṇic legend that has just been recalled, the behavior of Kāvya Uśanas and that of his mother, called on to stand in for him, are very different; while he (and this is what explains his absence) has gone off to see Śiva in order to ask him for a "victory formula" in the war that his clients are waging against the gods, his mother, as soon as she is placed at the head of the demons, botches up the situation by an excessive and bungling strategy: attacking the very kingship of Indra, setting fire to the world of the gods, she violates the tacit agreement by which the general staffs of any two warring parties refrain from certain excesses, and she provokes the always fearsome intervention of Viṣṇu, who cuts off her head. Then there is the risk of overpowering desires and emotions; these are jointly illustrated, in the two tales composed by the Indians and the Iranians after their separation, starting from ancient notions, by the equally unbridled passions of the daughter of Kāvya Uśanas and the wife of Kay Ūs. One will note that what the two tales emphasize most of all as the result of these irregularities is the disorder they cause in the normal transmission of power (political or magical) from man to man: the son of the king Kavi Usa(δa)n does not become the king that he ought to have been by birthright; the student of the kavi-magician Uśanas does not revive the dead as he should have done by virtue of the teaching he received.

VII

THE MAKING OF A DYNASTY

1. THE KAYANIDS—A HISTORICAL DYNASTY?

Even bearing in mind the accordances that we have tried to unravel in the preceding chapter, the fact remains that the Indian and Iranian narratives have nothing in common in their organization and the relative importance of the episodes: whether in terms of the nature and conduct of the main character or of the kavi society, the various comparisons have revealed only features, introduced and illustrated in distinctly different ways on each side. And let us not forget that besides the story in the first book of the *Mahābhārata* and the one that the *Xvatāy Nāmak* supplied to the interpreters of the "national tradition," a number of other traits external to the plot are attested, from the *ṚgVeda* to the Purāṇas on the one hand, and in the systematization of the history of the Kayanids on the other.

But what we have learned from these comparative reflections enables us to approach the problem differently from the way it was treated by Arthur Christensen (which is still common), who, after having discussed the data of the surviving *Avesta* and before considering the existing evidence of the Sassanian period, raised the question at the end of the second chapter of his book and summed it up, without looking outside of Iran, in a few words: "Is the period of the kavis mythic or historical?"[1] Historical, he answered, basing his conclusion on the following four, as he terms them, "facts":

(1) There is a fundamental difference between the eight kavis and the kings who precede them in the scheme of the Yašts—Haošyaŋha, Taxma Urupi, and Yima: while the latter are clearly "mythical or legendary" (dragon slayer, etc.), the kavis accomplish—except for an accretion of mythic traits borrowed from the Tricephalus in the parts concerning their Turanian adversary Fraŋrasyan—only "heroic, altogether human exploits"; "the fact that traditions subsequent to the Yašts have fleshed out the history of Kavi Usaδan and Kavi Haosravah with mythical episodes should not mislead us," as even the later and certainly historical figures have taken on "supernatural" traits.

(2) The first kings, certainly mythical, never receive the title of kavi, peculiar to the eastern Iranians and historically assured as a royal title for petty kings of the Zoroastrian period.

(3) The names of several of the eight kavis—Aršan, Byaršan, Syāvaršan—are of a pre-Zoroastrian type, which is to be expected for a dynasty which undoubtedly preceded, even if not by much, the Zoroastrian teachings.

(4) If we allow, as later tradition tells and as is probably true, that the four kavis from Kavi Usaδan (the third) to Kavi Byaršan (the sixth) are not fathers and sons but brothers, "one may assume" that these four kavis had first reigned independently over four separate territories, which were subsequently subdued by one of them, Kavi Usaδan (of whom the Yašts say that "he reigned over all the lands, over men and the demons"), and passed on to the last kavi, his grandson Haosravah.

Here is the picture that Christensen proposes:[2]

> After all, it would not be overbold to assume that the line of kavis gives us a historical outline spanning the period from

[1] *Les Kayanides*, pp. 27–35.
[2] Ibid.

the settling of Aryan immigrants in eastern Iran under an ordered monarchic regime to the Zoroastrian reform.

If we accept this reasoning, the information that we can draw from the Yašts will have some value in elucidating the otherwise unknown history of eastern Iran in pre-Achaemenian times. Faced with accounts which claim to be historical, and whose general character does not necessarily preclude a historical reality, the sound method is, in my view, not to seek myths in them at all costs, but to consider these accounts as having at least a basis in truth and to examine them in light of the psychological laws of the formation of legends.

In the lands located between the central deserts of Iran and the Indus basin, the Aryan tribes, coming from the north, established a monarchy under kings designated by the title "kavi." One of these kavis, Usaδan, united under his rule all the Aryan territory; it could have been said of him what *Yašt* 10 (13–14) says poetically of Mithra, that he "looked out over all the Aryan habitat where the great waters roll their waves toward Iškata and Puruta, towards Margiana, Aria, Gava (Sogdiana) and Khorasmia." He had a powerful enemy: Fraŋrasyan, the great chief of the Turanian tribes, who was also, probably, of Aryan race. The latter, having put to death Syāvaršan, the son of Usaδan, and another important personage, Ağraēraϑa of the Naravid family, succeeded in getting hold of the "xvarənah of the kavis," which is to say making himself a kavi, and lording it over the Aryans he fought and put to death a bitter enemy of theirs, whom tradition calls by a seemingly Iranian name, Zainigav. But Haosravah, son of Syāvaršan, rose against Fraŋrasyan and wrested the power from him. Fraŋrasyan attempted several times in vain to win back the divine Glory, which according to Iranian belief accompanies only legitimate kings, but a few great battles, which took place in a wooded region, brought an end to the war: Fraŋrasyan was defeated along with Kərəsavazdah, who was the mainstay of his throne, and both of them were put in chains and killed to avenge the murders of Syāvaršan and Ağraēraϑa. This epic war made an indelible impression on people's minds, and before long legend began to embellish the usurper with traits that seem to have been borrowed from the dragon-man Aži Dahāka.

With Haosravah, the glorious days of the kavis seem to have ended. There remained the memory of a son of Haosravah, Āxrūra, who had not borne the title of kavi. In the ensuing period the eastern lands were apparently dominated by petty kings who called themselves kavis. Among them was Kavi Vištāspa, the convert and protector of Zoroaster.

2. EXAMINATION OF ARTHUR CHRISTENSEN'S ARGUMENTS

From the moment Christensen published it, this picture and the methodology used to support it should have given rise to numerous objections regarding both details and principle. First of all, of the four "facts" which are invoked in support of it, some are inexactly presented and the rest do not necessarily lead to the conclusions that we are asked to draw.

(1) Neither the first three kings in the "scheme of the Yašts" nor the heroes Θraētaona and Kərəsāspa are any "more mythical" than the kavis; they simply have more fantastic and especially more detailed and picturesque myths than those with which the Yašts credit the only two kavis, Usaδan and Haosravah, about whom they give any details. About the first, under the short form of the name, Usan, we learn simply that he was a man of prodigious strength (*Yašt* 14, 39) and that he attained to the highest power over all the lands, over all men and the demons (*Yašt* 5, 45–47). By conjuring away the demons in his historical reconstruction, Christensen sees in these last words merely a figurative expression meaning that a historical king by the name of Kavi Usaδan had united eastern Iran. The Yašts say nothing more of Haošyaŋha, the first "mythical" king, beyond breaking down and expanding on each item: Haošyaŋha asks the Goddess of Waters (*Yašt* 5, 21),

> "Grant me this fortune . . . that I may attain supreme sovereignty over all lands, over demons and men, over sorcerers and tyrants, kavis and karapans, that I may overthrow two-thirds of the Mazanian demons and the Varənian miscreants!"

With a slight variation, he asks the Goddess Drvāspā (*Yašt* 9, 4):

> "Grant me this fortune . . . that I may be the conqueror of all the Mazanian demons, that I may not take flight in fear of the demons, but that all the demons may flee in terror, despite themselves, and plunge full of fear into the darkness!"

And the three other Yašts which have him address prayers to Vayu (*Yašt* 15, 12) and to Aši Vaŋuhī (*Yašt* 15, 25) or mention his successes (*Yašt* 19, 26) simply repeat one or the other of these formulas. By what criteria does one decide that victory "over all men and demons" is a mythical representation when it refers to Haošyaŋha, and that it is only a metaphor, embellishment, or expression of the "formulaic language of the Yašts" when it refers to a kavi?

(2) The established "fact" is limited to this: that the shift of the term kavi in the sense of a political chief, king, is peculiar to eastern Iran, hence the narratives of the kavi-kings—whether mythical or historical—must have originated in this part of Iran.

(3) That three of the names of the kavis have pre-Zoroastrian forms only leads one to believe that, mythical or historical, they do in fact antedate Zoroaster.

(4) Clearly, this is not a matter of fact, but an assumption that already implies as given what it was intended to prove.

As for the methodology—the reconstruction of historical facts based on legends of which one retains only those parts that are "reasonable" or "likely" and discards the rest—this is a game as easy as it is arbitrary, and therefore useless. Moreover, one would really like to know these "psychological laws of legend formation" which make it possible thus to extract objectively "a basis in truth"

—perhaps these laws will exist some day, but at the present stage of studies in this field, they serve only to mask with high-sounding language the preferences of the critic.

Actually, Christensen sidestepped the true problem, which should have preceded his initial remarks and which is comparative and simple to state: does comparison reveal, between the Iranian Kay Ūs and his Indic near-homonym, the assuredly mythical Kāvya Uśanas, any accordances that cannot be explained either by chance or by borrowing by India from Iran, or does it not? If the answer is negative, the way is clear for Christensen's undertaking, with all the risks involved; if the answer is positive, the attempt is doomed from the start, because then Kay Ūs is himself a mythical figure inserted into history. We know now that such accordances do exist. They are too numerous, too specific, and too peculiar to be explained by accident. On the other hand, borrowing by India from Iran is excluded, since it is India that has preserved the ancient, magico-religious sense of the term *kaví*, considerably transformed in Iran. Finally, a borrowing in the other direction is no more acceptable, because the accordances pertain not to what is readily borrowed, namely connected narratives, but to character traits and behavior patterns which have been staged and elaborated differently by the Indians and the Iranians.

This conclusion entails considerable consequences. First of all, it confirms once again that, over and above the silence or the meager selection of information contained in the most ancient texts, in both India and Iran, more recent and sometimes late texts have preserved, resetting them in contemporary style, features whose similarities compel us to assign them to the period of Indo-Iranian unity. Thus it is necessary to correct accordingly the evolutionary perspective proposed by Christensen: the "innovations" that the Pahlavi texts and the epic of the Islamic period attribute to Kay Ūs are not new except in form, in dress, in plot—in reality they preserve pre-Zoroastrian material. The problem is no longer to find out from where the principal pieces of this material have been drawn (those that we have just seen to be common to these texts and the *Mahābhārata*), but why the preserved parts of the *Avesta*, particularly the Yašts, passed over them in silence.

Second, it is not only this theme, these traits, these patterns of action of Kay Ūs which are of "mythical" (or to put it more modestly, legendary) origin, it is the character himself—it would be acrobatic to accept that there existed, within a dynasty of kavi-kings, a real man by the name of Kavi Usa(δa)n like the legendary Indo-Iranian *Kavi Uśan, whose real type and history were forgotten and then replaced by the traditional type and legend of this homonym. If one were to persist in regarding the kavi dynasty as basically historical, it would be more plausible to think that, toward the middle of that dynasty, those in charge of "history" had inserted, with his name, his character, and his deeds, some famous kavi who belonged to the realm of saga.

3. OTHER MYTHICAL THEMES IN THE HISTORY OF THE KAYANIDS: THE HERO IN THE WATER REED

But—and this is the third subject of reflection that comes to mind—is it really a question of a flagrant interpolation of the legendary into the historical? Is it not on the contrary the whole kavi dynasty that by implication becomes suspect as being nothing but historicized legend?

Admittedly this can be proven only in the case of Kavi Usa(δa)n: the other dynastic names are peculiar to Iran, and are not to be found in Indian onomastics, either real or legendary, except for the name of the last kavi, Haosravah, which is matched in the Vedas and the *Mahābhārata* by several Suśrávās, about whom what little is said does not lend itself to any comparison with what we know of Haosravah. But this name, which means "having good glory, very glorious" and which would be in Greek Εὐκλεής, was so easy to form and so trite that it does not demand the hypothesis of a common origin, unlike the complex accordance of the Vedic Kāvya (kavi) Uśanas and the Avestan Kavi Usan. Nonetheless, alerted by the case of the latter, we should pay careful attention to what is said of the other kavis in the same texts, Pahlavi and Persian, which have been found to be so conservative in the case of Kay Ūs. For several of these texts tell, and tell nothing but, marvelous things that one no longer dares characterize, without further examination, as "late additions" or "embellishments."

One of the first ones concerns an identifiable mythical theme whose Indo-Iranian character has been established for a long time, by the demonstration of a parallel between an episode in the *Mahābhārata* and an Armenian narrative which both present the same divine figure.[3] It involves the god of victory, Indra *Vṛtrahán*, "slayer of Vṛtra" (or "smasher of obstructions") in India; *Vahagn* in Armenia; that is, under a form borrowed from Middle Iranian, the *Vərəϑrağna* of Iran. The *Mahābhārata* recounts how, between his victory over Vṛtra and the consecration that one would think this should have earned him immediately, Indra disappears, and takes up residence, in miniature form, in the stalk of a lotus that lies on an island in the middle of the ocean. The fire god has to find him, then the priest of the gods must chant over him and "reinflate" him, and only then does he come out triumphantly from the stalk, not before having instituted a sacrifice in which fire and himself are intimately associated. A song fragment from Zoroastrianized Armenia recounts the birth of Vahagn: in a stream of smoke and flame, he springs forward in the shape of a young man with fiery hair, out of a reed stalk situated in the middle of the sea, and he begins his career as the "strangler of dragons," *višapakał*.

In Indo-Iranian times this spectacular epiphany, birth or rebirth, surely belonged to Indra Vṛtrahan. But we know that Indra was one of the main victims of the Zoroastrian reform. He became one of the arch-demons diametrically opposed to the archangels, and his role of warrior, rehabilitated, moralized, and placed in the service of the true religion, was divided between the traditional god Mithra, untroublesome for the reformers, and the personified abstraction of victory, Vərəϑrağna, in whom the title of the fallen

[3] *The Destiny of the Warrior*, pp. 121–123.

god transparently survived. The Armenian legend of Vahagn proves that in certain forms of Zoroastrianism the theme of warrior-god waiting inside the water reed for the hour of his manifestation was passed on as such to Vərəϑraǧna. This is not the case in strict Zoroastrianism, such as is expressed in the preserved *Avesta* and in the Pahlavi summaries of the lost parts of the Sassanian *Avesta*. Nonetheless, the theme was not suppressed. It was only lowered from the divine to the heroic level, and complicated by being combined with a mythical concept peculiar to the Iranians, but very important to all the peoples of the family, even the Scythians, and thus pre-Zoroastrian: that of x^{v}*arənah* (Middle Iranian *xvarrah*), itself closely linked to victory, especially to Vərəϑraǧna. The x^{v}arənah, for a prince and upon a prince, is a visible mark, the sign and warranty of favor, or better, of divine election. No doubt artificially, the *Bundahišn* distinguishes three forms of the xvarrah, that of the kavi-kings, that of the Iranians, and that of the priests. In any case, the x^{v}arənah has the peculiarity of transferring itself, or rather passing by the will of God, from one elect whose term is up to another who is beginning his, as well as of withdrawing from an elect who has become unworthy.

It is thus that the x^{v}arənah of Θraētaona (Pahlavi Frētōn), conqueror of the Tricephalus—in which role he has replaced the Indo-Iranian *Trita and corresponds to the Vedic Trita, Indra's helper or substitute in the murder of the Tricephalus—is kept in reserve for another beneficiary, who will be the second, if not the founder, of the dynasty of the kavi-kings: Kavi Aipivohu, Pahlavi Kay Apivēh. In what form? The account of the *Bundahišn*, which offers the only known tradition about this kavi, is complex and obscure on more than one point, but clear on the one that is important to us.[4]

> The xvarrah of Frētōn had lodged in the roots of a reed, in the ocean Frāxvkart. By sorcery Nōtargā transformed a

[4] 35.38 (Trans. adapted from Anklesaria, p. 299). On certain elements of the story (the elimination of the sons, the choosing of the daughter, the milk) see *The Destiny of a King*, pp. 80–81, 104.

> cow into a goat and took it there. He harvested the reeds, and for a year he fed the cow on them so that the xvarrah passed into the cow. He took the cow back to his place, milked it, and gave the milk to his three sons, Vāmūn, Šun, and Changraŋhā. But the xvarrah did not enter his sons, but went into Frāna [his daughter]. Nōtargā wished to kill Frāna; she escaped from her father, thanks to the xvarrah, and she vowed to give her first child to Ušbām. Thus Ušbām saved her from her father. The first child that she bore was Kay Apivēh, whom she gave to Ušbām. She remained with Ušbām as his companion.

We are thus amid the miraculous, and the first occasion of this marvel—the others remaining unexplained—answers the problem arising from the Indo-Iranian tradition concerning the method of either the rebirth or birth of the god of victory, and does so in a way that is imposed by the nature of the x^varənah: "How, with a view to its reuse for the benefit of one newly chosen, to get the x^varənah of a victorious hero out of the water reed where it has withdrawn?"

Thus the second kavi too, like the sixth, seems to have profited from a history fabricated from ancient, partially Indo-Iranian myths: the historicity of the dynasty as such is not strengthened by this. If one insists on it, one can maintain the possibility that a line of kavi-kings did exist, even under the names given them by "history" (except, of course, Kavi Usa[δa]n, caught red-handed in historical unreality right down to his name), and that the real events of their reigns, their true characteristics, and so on, were entirely covered over and replaced by the more prestigious preexistent legendary material. This complication seems, in my view, both groundless and unnecessary.

4. THE PROHIBITION OF DRUNKENNESS

It will be necessary to widen this inquiry to all the kavis as they are presented, occasionally with new details, by the texts of the Islamic period, starting from the *Xvatāy Nāmak* or other lost Pahlavi sources. Other Indo-Iranian parallels will undoubtedly appear, other myths or historicized legends will come to light. I will cite but one example, involving the first member of the dynasty, Kavi Kavāta, and once again the Indian Kāvya Uśanas.

In the Yašts, Kavi Kavāta is no more than a name. The *Bundahišn* attaches to him a theme frequent in legends of founders:[5] a distant descendant of Manuščihr, therefore of Frētōn, by the name of Uzāv, saw one day a baby shivering with cold in a basket abandoned on a river. He took it, raised it, and named it "the foundling." Nothing is said of his reign, only that he was the father of Kay Apivēh[6] (though it is hard to see how, considering the story that we have just read about the latter's birth). The writers of Islamic times fabricated a reign for him out of commonplace elements: towns constructed, named, and made prosperous; digging of canals; and the institution of milestones and of tithing (Belʿamī). Only al-Thaʿālibī attributes to him a more specific adventure:[7]

> One day, standing on the terrace of one of his palaces and contemplating the green fields that spread all around him, his eyes as far as they could see beheld nothing but greenery. While he feasted his eyes on the beauty of the scene, enchanted by the visible proof of cultivation, he spotted far away in a gap in the verdure something black on white. Having given orders to send a man there immediately to bring him an explanation of this, the messenger upon his return reported that a man going from one village to another, totally drunk, had fallen in the field like a dead body, and that a raven had swooped on him and plucked out his eyes. Kay Kobād, badly shaken by this, decreed a prohibition on wine drinking and a most severe punishment against offenders. And the people abstained from drinking wine for a certain time.
>
> Now it happened one day that a lion had escaped from the menagerie, and no one was able to stop it or bring it back

[5] 35.28 (Anklesaria, pp. 296–297).

[6] 35.29 (ibid.).

[7] *Histoire des Rois des Perses*, pp. 149–152.

until a young man who was passing through grabbed it by the ears, mounted it like a donkey and made it walk about tamely, then delivered it to its guardians. His adventure was reported to Kay Kobād, who was greatly astounded by it and said: "The young man must either be a fool or drunk." He had him brought to him and said: "Let me know, without lying, how you could be so brave as to approach the lion and mount it, and you will be exempt from all blame." The young man replied: "Know, O King, that I love a cousin who is to me the most precious thing in the world. I had my uncle's promise that he would give her to me in marriage, but he broke his word and married her to someone else, because of my humble situation in life and my poverty. When I was told of this, I was on the point of killing myself and my despair was extreme. Well, my mother, who took pity on me, said: 'This, my son, is a grief that you cannot conquer except with three cups of wine, which will comfort you a bit.' 'How can I drink wine,' I said to her, 'considering the king's interdiction?' She said to me: 'Drink in hiding, need legitimizes what is forbidden; besides, who would inform on you?' Well, I had a few cups after having eaten some *kebab*, and came out with all the strength of wine, youth, and love, and I did my deed with the lion." The king was greatly astonished. He sent for the young man's uncle and ordered him to annul the marriage of his son-in-law and his daughter, and to marry her to his nephew. The uncle complied and Kay Kobād made him a present. The king took on the young man as his retainer and helped him overcome his destitution. Then he addressed the people with the following proclamation: "Drink all the wine you need to get in the spirit of chasing a lion, but be careful not to drink yourselves into a state where the ravens could pluck out your eyes!" The people then went back to their habit of drinking wine, but avoided complete drunkenness.

We recognize here a widespread theme in the folklore of alcoholic beverages: for one reason or another, a king bans its use; someone violates the prohibition, is brought before the king, and saves his life by his wits; sometimes the prohibition is also repealed or moderated. In the Near East the story is attributed to various sultans,[8] but a variant has been noted as far north as Scandinavia. Saxo Grammaticus recounts that, in the time of the legendary King Snio, a long spell of bad weather had ruined the harvest and caused a famine.[9] Having observed that more grain was consumed in beer than in food (*cum aliquanto maiorem bibulorum quam edacium impensam animaduerteret*), the king banned all beer drinking (*conuiuiorum usum abrogans*), and forbade even the brewing of it. The people complied, except one, *quidam petulantioris gulae*, who three times, thanks to stratagems of an amusing subtlety (*a ridiculi operis acumine*), circumvented the decree and justified himself before the king. First, instead of "drinking," he "licked" the beer; then he "had the beer drunk" by some tarts (*crustulis*), which he in turn "ate," thus getting drunk indirectly (*capace liquoris offula uescebatur cupitamque crapulum lento gustu prouexit*); finally he started drinking publicly, and when the king questioned him for the last time he explained that it was out of pity for him, the king, that he continued to brew beer despite the prohibition, so that on the day of the royal funeral there would be no lack of ferment for the beer for the indispensable funeral drinking. This irony (*cauillatio*) put the king to shame, and he lifted the ban.

But let us return to Iran: the reign of the first kavi is thus marked by the prohibition of wine, onto which has been grafted a folkloric variant justifying the softening of the ban. One can by no means maintain that there is anything whatever historical in the anecdote, but it may be that the kavi type excluded the abuse or use of alcoholic beverages. In fact, in India it is to Kāvya Uśanas that the *Mahābhārata* attributes without reversal or attenuation the prohibition of the intoxicant *surā*, which only concerns, it is true, those of his own social class, the brahmins (remembering that

[8] E.g. in one of my "Récits Oubykh III," *Journal Asiatique* 247 (1959), pp. 167–170.

[9] *Gesta Danorum* 8.11, 12; Peter Fisher (trans.), *History of the Danes* (Cambridge, 1979), pp. 259–260.

Kāvya Uśanas, and with him the kavi type, was standardized as a brahmin in the epic). Indeed, it is in surā that his employers the demons made him drink the ashes of his disciple Kaca to prevent him from applying to him his "life science." The result was his own death, bracketed by two resurrections. Once recovered from this ordeal, he took out his anger first on the surā: having experienced for himself the "destruction of consciousness" (*saṃjñānāśa*) which it causes, he resolved to protect the brahmins against this risk, and pronounced a curse against any of them who from that day on allowed themselves to be led astray into drinking: their transgression would be considered as serious, with consequences as heavy in this world as in the other, as the most abominable crime of all, the killing of a brahmin.

This little scene is all the more remarkable as there has been no hint in the preceding events of any loss of consciousness or drunkenness: the demons could have mixed up the ashes in any colored drink, and Kāvya has sized up the situation with his daughter with a completely cool head. Besides, for the institution of this prohibition the Indian pundits could have found, among their innumerable mythical candidates including ṛṣis of all sorts, a safer and more strictly sacerdotal bet than this wizard, the chaplain of the demons. If they ascribe it to him in this passage, which contains so many elements of a very ancient legend, it is undoubtedly because they have been faithful to tradition. One is thus led to believe that the Indian epic has either preserved or added to the endowment of its kavi par excellence a truly "kavic" feature, one that certain Iranian scholars made use of on their side to beef up the uneventful reign of the first in their long line of kavis.

5. KAY ŪS AND SRĪT

Last, it seems possible to demonstrate in the saga of Kay Ūs itself the Indo-Iranian origin of an episode whose Indic equivalent is not furnished by the story of Kāvya Uśanas.

It was recalled in the Introduction[10] that besides Θraētaona, Iran already in the *Avesta* had preserved a Θrita, whose name exactly matches that of the Indic Trita, although the latter's Iranian counterpart in terms of action is Θraētaona; furthermore, this Avestan Θrita was apparently invested with a medical function—he was effective against demonic sicknesses created by the Evil Spirit. It was also recalled at the time that, in Vedic ritual and in the etiological myths, Trita is charged with disburdening man of certain taints: he takes them onto himself and gets rid of them by transferring them to great sinners, and eventually to the perpetrators of unforgivable sins. These taints are those that result from otherwise useful and necessary killings: in myth, that of the Tricephalus (from which he frees Indra); in ritual, that of the sacrificial victim (from which he frees the sacrificer).

In the expected form of Srīt, the Avestan Θrita continues to exist in the Pahlavi books. He has actually been split into three, and one of these Srīts, in an episode during the reign of the ambivalent Kay Ūs, plays a role that brings to mind that played by Trita, the scapegoat of Indra: he is the scapegoat of the king.[11]

As Zoroastrianism no longer allows animal sacrifices, it is in connection with the criminal killing of a miraculous ox, and not the necessary killing of a sacrificial one, that he steps in. In order to settle the disputes over the drawing of their boundary lines, the Iranians and the Turanians referred the case to an ox who marked out the correct boundary with his hoof. Resentful of the authority of this eminently mithraic animal, and egged on by the demons as he repeatedly was in the course of his reign, Kay Ūs decided to kill it, and sent for that purpose one of his officers named Srīt, "the seventh of seven brothers" (this detail being no doubt a trace of the name's ordinal value, "third of three, last of three," at a stage of the language when the form Srīt no longer connoted either the cardinal number three or the ordinal third). When he got near him,

[10] Above, p. 2.

[11] *Zātspram* 4.9–26; *Dēnkart* 7.2.61–66. Molé, *La légende de Zoroastre selon les textes pehlevis*, pp. 24–26; *The Destiny of the Warrior*, p. 27, n. 22.

the ox admonished him in a human voice, which disconcerted him to such an extent that he returned to the king and requested confirmation of the order. The order was confirmed and Srīt went to kill the ox. But as soon as he did so his soul was overcome with unbearable turmoil, and returning again to the king, he asked to be killed.

> "Why should I kill you," replied Kay Ūs, "since it is not you who wanted this?"
>
> "If you do not kill me," said the officer, "I shall kill you."
>
> "Do not kill me, for I am monarch of the world" (*dēhpat i gēhān*).

Because Srīt was so insistent, the king sent him to a place where a sorceress lived in the form of a dog who, when Srīt struck her with his sword, became double; the sorceresses kept multiplying in this way at every blow, and when there were a thousand of them, Srīt was torn apart and died.

The king's sin, claimed by the king, is thus taken on by the executioner Srīt, just as the sin of the Indian god is assumed by his helper Trita. Filled with sorrow, seeking a death that seems to end his defilement, Srīt expiates the murder for which the king, in any case, suffers no punishment, not even spiritual. Trita, more of an expert, knows how to rid himself of the taint from which he has previously freed the god (or the sacrificer) by passing it on to great sinners. The motives behind both transfers are similar, and the analogy is underlined by the words of the two accounts: "Indra was surely free [of the sin] because he is god," explains *Śatapatha Brāhmaṇa* 1.2.3.2, and "Do not kill me," says Kay Ūs himself to his justicer, "for I am monarch of the world."

The "historians" who busied themselves with embellishing the reign of the great kavi have chosen this subject sagaciously: expanding on a type of Indo-Iranian sorcerer who maneuvered between the gods and the demons, Kay Ūs, a king, oscillates constantly, as we have seen, between good and evil, and commits sins that God would not have allowed to go unpunished in any other case. It was tempting to incorporate into his story an episode that illustrated his malicious side, but where a traditional scapegoat accounted for his long impunity.

6. PROBLEMS

The subject of the Kayanids is not fully covered by the foregoing remarks, but they suffice perhaps to dissuade us from seeking there the embellished recollection of real events. After this, two problems, which will not be dealt with here, present themselves.

One concerns the soldering of the purely legendary history of Iran, thus considerably drawn out, to the actual history with all its distortions of persons and events known to us from other sources (such as the period of the Achaemenids reduced to two Dārās, or the period of Iskender and his successors). As always in similar cases, it is a difficult problem to solve.[12] In Rome it is under the fourth king, Ancus Marcius, that we begin to discern the first traces of authentic facts: the development and organization of the plebs, exposure to the influence and soon the domination of the Etruscans. But even these facts do not guarantee that there was a king by that name; this could have been imposed on the compilers of the early history by the *gens Marcia*, who were active and ambitious in the fourth century. As for the Scandinavian Ynglingar and Skjöldungar, the uncertainty is much greater and few critics dare commit themselves. Similarly, debate will go on about Iran for a long time, I fear, with the aggravating circumstance that the beginnings of Zoroastrianism are bound up in the matter. Is it in the person of Kavi Haosravah that we touch upon historical reality, despite the legend of his birth and the entirely mythical intervention of his fravaši in the life of his mythical grandfather? Was Kavi Vištāspa, the protector of Zoroaster, really the Vištāspa whom the "national tradition" gives as the second successor to Kavi Haosravah? If this is accepted, then how is one to explain the structure

[12] Wikander, "Sur le fonds commun indo-iranien des épopées de la Perse et de l'Inde" (see above, p. 8, n. 17), pp. 310–329, especially p. 321.

that Wikander has uncovered in the grouping of these last pre-Achaemenian kings?[13]

The second, twofold problem concerns the two extremely long-lived beings or groups of beings who give color and unity to the Kayanid period: on one side the Sistanian heroes, Zāl and Rustam, and on the other the Turanian Afrāsyāb. In both cases, the legendary and even mythical interpretations, already suggested by the data themselves, become even more plausible now that the kings whom these heroes serve or fight against are themselves amenable to such an interpretation. Zāl and Rustam have already been considered in this light, but there is reason to reexamine Fraŋrasyan/Afrāsyāb, who is presented at one time as a king (and a useful one) of Iran, and about whom it is not enough to say with Christensen that "before long legend began to embellish the usurper with traits that seem to have been borrowed from the dragon-man Aži Dahāka." It is rather in the well-stocked bazaar of Indic demons, Vedic or epic, that one should search for his brother.[14]

[13] Ibid. pp. 324–326.

[14] [1982] On the mythicality or historicity of the Kayanids, see now Jean Kellens, "L'Avesta comme source historique: la liste des Kayanides," *Acta Asiatica Academiae Scientiarum Hungaricae* 24 (1976), pp. 37–49. Kellens essentially agrees with me, with one reservation (p. 42, n. 8). On Xšaϑra, see the same author's "L'Iran réformé ou les malheurs du guerrier," in the volume that Pandora Editions and Centre Georges Pompidou have recently devoted to my work, *Georges Dumézil* (*Cahiers pour un temps* [1981]), pp. 159–172. Personally, I still believe that Xšaϑra, who fills the slot of *Indra in the list of Archangels that replaced the Indo-Iranian divinities of the three functions, must have preserved, separate from the abstract speculations preserved only in the *Gāthās*, the warlike nature of his prototype (confirmed by the Vedic and Scythian data), and that this preserved character appears later, for example on coins. In the same way, beneath the abstractions (in the form of feminine nouns) Haurvatāt and Amərətāt, "Wholeness" and "Non-death," the twin *Nāhatyas must have survived, since the two (quite masculine!) angels who bear their names in Judeo-Islamic angelology, Hārūt and Mārūt, are still the protagonists of an adventure story that is close to one of the principal Vedic Nāsatya myths. See my *Dieux souverains des Indo-Européens* (Paris, 1977), pp. 40–51, especially p. 46, n. 1.

PROSPECTUS

Just as Herman Lommel in 1939 rediscovered and made fruitful (after half a century of *Ignorierung*) Friedrich von Spiegel's hypothesis on Kāvya Uśanas and Kavi Usan, so Stig Wikander in 1959, in his article in *La Nouvelle Clio,* "Sur le fonds commun indo-iranien des épopées de la Perse et de l'Inde,"[1] confirmed and enriched the remarks James Darmesteter had made in 1887 in his article entitled "Points de contact entre le Mahābhārata et le Shāh Nāmeh."[2] It is perhaps of some interest to point out that in studies of comparative Indo-European grammar too there was to be a wait of more than a half century until, beyond Karl Brugmann and Antoine Meillet, the rigorous boldness of the *Mémoire* of Ferdinand de Saussure (1878) would inspire the *Études* of Jerzy Kuryłowicz (1935) and Émile Benveniste's *Origines* (1935). In the maturation that extracts new disciplines from the nebula, such an alternation between advance and retreat is normal, and it is not overly optimistic to say that nothing is ever lost of propositions that are ahead of their time—they only await, in the vast and timeless depths of libraries, the browsing curiosity or the searching restlessness of a free spirit.

Darmesteter and Wikander have therefore established that rare epic themes occur jointly in the *Mahābhārata* and in the *Shāh Nāmeh,* in such detail that borrowing is improbable in either direction. Wikander has shown further that the ideology of the three functions, in varying shape and scope, has served in both epics to

[1] Above, p. 8, n. 17; p. 105, n. 12.

[2] *Journal Asiatique* 2 (1887): 38–75.

structure the material. Finally, the study of Kavi Usan that we have just made has rendered it probable that this king, one of the two most substantial Kayanids, and with him all of the Kayanid kings, are not historical figures that have been retouched in various degrees, but spring from historicized mythical conceptions and representations that the Indic Kāvya Uśanas enables us to pin down. It will be up to the following generations of researchers to push the comparison, certainly farther than we can envisage. Not with the intent of dictating the course of future development but to spare it some wasted effort, it would be wise to make explicit here, next to the concordances already recognized, a more fundamental difference: the *Mahābhārata* and the *Shāh Nāmeh* were not created for the same purpose; their frameworks, the guidelines according to which they dispose and organize partially shared material, are not congruent.

The *Mahābhārata* is not the history of one or of several dynasties. More precisely, it presents in its introduction (that is, in a few sections of the first book) the ancestors of the two groups of protagonists. Symmetrically, at the other end of the poem, in the fourteenth and seventeenth books, we witness the birth of the wonder child, Parikṣit, and Yudhiṣṭhira's cession of the throne to him, thus assuring, after the retreat and death of the protagonists, the rebirth of the dynasty and the restarting of the mechanism of generations and successions. But in the body of the poem it is only the protagonists' generation that is spoken of, from the second part of the first book where Yudhiṣṭhira and his brothers and cousins are born and grow up to the last pages of the eighteenth book, where Yudhiṣṭhira meets his cousins and brothers in paradise for the final reconciliation.

If, then, sticking literally to its title—"The Great History of the Bhāratas"—we were to accept that the subject of the poem is the dynasty per se, the succession of fathers and sons, the detailing of events and rules that assure its continuity down through the centuries—in short the divine scheme that begins with the first ancestor and remains open-ended after the accession of Parikṣit, then the *Mahābhārata* would appear to be an organism as out of balance as man himself, every person, every animal seen from the perspective of evolution: the essence of each of us, the reason we are here, lies in a few reproductive cells and minor organs, a semen pouch or a uterus, with which we fulfill more or less regularly our duty as perpetuators of the species through time. And yet from these trifling things sprout all the actors of the fable of Menenius Agrippa (Livy 2.32), from the skeleton to the neurons (and, alas, to the wrinkles of fat), all this confounded body that makes our unhappiness, our good fortune, our folly, and shares in the follies, the happiness and unhappiness of our innumerable contemporaries, as transitory as ourselves. It is the same with the *Mahābhārata*, looked at from the genealogist's standpoint: almost from the start the succession of begettings is halted; the great adventure of a single generation places it on hold and even jeopardizes its future, as the men do battle through many cantos, instead of being content for a while, like their predecessors, each with his own bed and the adjoining nursery. Thus we must take another point of view: if we prefer individuals to the race as a whole, if the brains and muscles, morals and great feats of outstanding examples of humankind capture our imaginations more than the monotonous flow of generational sperm, then we shall not be sorry for this halt, this outgrowth, and, set back on its powerful feet, the poetic organism will cease to be a monster.

The Iranian *Book of Kings* offers, in the main, a reverse satisfaction: there are long series of reigns, many of them characterized poorly, if not sketchily, whereas a few of them form small novelettes. Each one is self-contained, or at most two or three make up a limited whole: for example, when a son inherits a vendetta or is called upon to redress a situation compromised by his father. What gives some coherence to these occasionally extensive units is the assurance of a divine design, the appearance of a Providence—Zoroastrian before Islam, simply theistic in the Islamic writers—that protects, punishes, and never forsakes; it is consequently an almost biblical feeling that guided in this way, eternal Iran has preserved its nobility and its luck even in the times of its gravest trials.

But this sentiment grows out of the many shifts in perspective which necessarily go along with changes in ruling power: *gesta Dei per Persas*. This is true of the historical periods, sometimes extensively retouched ad hoc: the Achaemenids, Alexander, the Arsacids, the Sassanians. It is also true of everything, from the first man to the last of the Kayanids, that preceded the ghostly figures of two Dariuses.

But the Iranian *Book of Kings* also, as we recalled at the end of the last chapter, carries a bulky excrescence, one of a different kind than the strife among the Indic cousins: collateral, not central. It does not interrupt the flow of the royal generations, it accompanies it. This is the Sistanian epic, that of the leaders of one of the eastern provinces of Iran, not of Iran itself, the two most remarkable of whom are Zāl and his son Rustam, who are for many years the devoted and efficient upholders of the throne of the "king of kings." The two parallel histories and the lives of men in the two dynasties have neither the same rhythm nor the same time span: Zāl and Rustam lived several hundred years without losing (at least in Rustam's case) their strength or their martial valor, so that they find themselves successively the contemporaries and supporters of all the Kayanid kings, and they fall out with the central power and perish (Rustam at least by a trap) only under the "third-function kings," according to Wikander's analysis—under Bahman to be exact. If there were no more than this, it would still be only a matter of two juxtaposed Books of Kings, one national, the other provincial. But another strong unifying element comes into the picture, symmetrical with the Sistanian element: under so many kings, the principal exploits of Zāl and especially Rustam are accomplished at the expense of the Turanians, commanded from beginning to end by one and the same chieftain, as energetic and multicentenary as themselves, apparently a historicized demon, whom the *Avesta* calls Fraŋrasyan, the Pahlavi books Frāsiyāp, the Islamic writers Afrāsyāb. The attacks of Afrāsyāb begin even before the Kayanids, under the successors that Firdausi assigns to Feridūn. Consequently, distinct as they are, the reigns of these various kings, to the large extent that they consist of wars against the north, are less independent of each other than it seems at first: from Feridūn's great-grandson Manuščihr to Kai Xosrau we can speak of a unified "narrative of Afrāsyāb," of which the reigns of the kings of Iran only mark off the episodes.

We can now distinguish clearly the homologous parts of the two epics. It is not the whole of the *Shāh Nāmeh* (up to the Dārās) and the whole *Mahābhārata* (up to Parikṣit); it is the whole *Shāh Nāmeh* and the section of the introduction of the *Mahābhārata*, a minute fraction of the poem, in which the ancestors of the Pāṇḍavas are paraded from their beginnings: it is here that we find, and this is the extent of, what one might call the Indic Book of Kings.

Of course, the term "homologous" does not imply that these two lines of kings are superimposable. It simply means that we have a chance of finding there, incorporated and employed in places and functions often very different (such as Kāvya Uśanas and Kavi Usan), certain epic types, royal or not, going back to the Indo-Iranian unity and possibly even older.

But the parallelism does not go beyond these general coordinates. In particular, it does not enter into the patterns of dynastic composition.

The progression of pre-Achaemenid kings in Iran presents a simple structure. Multidynastic in the earliest documents and unified later on by artificial and sometimes uncertain family ties, it can be apportioned in some respects, as Wikander has shown, according to the framework of the three functions.

(1) After the cosmogonic figures comes a succession of three kings, bound up together in the Avestan version. Only the first one, strictly speaking, is the *Paraδāta*, "the one created before, as the first," but tradition quickly extended the title to all three, whom we call after the form taken later by this name—"Pishdadians." The task of these universal sovereigns, these "first kings," was a religious and organizational one: to civilize the world and to contend for it with the demons *qua* demons. They are, under their

Avestan names, Haošyaŋha Paraδāta, Taxma Urupi, and the most famous, Yima Xšaēta, the epic Jamšīd.

(2) After a confused period that the variants have filled out in various ways begins a line of kings of another type, the kavis or "Kayanids," whose mission is to defend Iran, to which their kingship is legally confined, against the aggressions of their neighbors, particularly those in the north, the Turanians. The last of the Kayanids in direct line temporarily puts an end to the fighting by killing the most formidable of these enemies. All this transposes into human terms mythic types and events. Still full of miracles, this period is essentially one of warfare.

(3) A few reigns conclude, in the epic, the list of the pre-Achaemenid kings. These are the reigns of Luhrāsp and Guštāsp, then Esfandiyār, then Bahman, then a woman, Humāy. Darmesteter had already noted the "difficulty of the *Avesta* and the epic in linking up Aurvataspa [= Luhrāsp] and Vištāspa [= Guštāsp] to the preceding dynasty, the Kayanids: Luhrāsp succeeds Kai Xosrau [the last Kayanid] no one knows why or how, and the Iranian nobles, like us, wonder where he comes from." Wikander has made some sound comments about these last sovereigns, in the light of Indic and Indo-Iranian mythology of the three functions, which make it probable that, coming after the Pishdadians and the Kayanids, they illustrate certain aspects of the third function:[3]

> The accession of Luhrāsp means not only a change of dynasty and capital [to Balch in Bactria], but a great change in the tenor and the subject matter of the narrative of the *Shāh Nāmeh*. The fantastic and supernatural events of the first epoch are followed by quieter times and more human circumstances. There are still wars, but the fantastic and the supernatural have disappeared. Women play a rather important role, and the last sovereign of this dynasty is in fact a woman. Nöldeke, who has expressly taken note of this "change of atmosphere," adds that only the adventures of Rustam are still marked by the supernatural and mythical element that prevails in earlier times.

[3] Wikander, "Sur le fonds commun," pp. 317–319.

One might maintain with some probability that this new atmosphere reflects the philosophy of the third estate. But most important, one would still have to wonder why it is precisely with Luhrāsp that "history" begins to reflect this ideology.

The name Nāhīd (= Anāhitā, wife of Guštāsp) is not the only thing that points to the myths. Luhrāsp (Aurvataspa) is named only once in the *Avesta*, as a worshipper of the goddess Anāhitā (*Yašt* 5, 105). Therefore, if Balch (which in reality was never the capital of Iran) appears at this point in the narrative, perhaps it is to pave the way for the legend of Zoroaster, but perhaps also because Balch and Bactria were famous for the temple of Anaitis, and because several figures of the legend of Zoroaster are known to us first as worshippers of this goddess.

Moreover, the relationship of Luhrāsp and Guštāsp is altogether peculiar. The first one accomplishes neither deed nor exploit; his entire reign is summed up in one conflict with his son and the son's trip to Rum (Byzantium) to win the Princess Kitāyūn-Nāhīd. Then he abdicates in favor of this son and retires to the temple of Balch. It is said that he and Guštāsp reigned one hundred and twenty years each—this is the only case where the same length of reign is attributed to two successive kings. One might add that these are the only cases where Iranian kings bear names composed with *aspa*, "horse."

Here we are in possession of data specific enough for us to begin to discern an Indo-European mythological theme: "the divine twins in the service of a goddess." The names Luhrāsp-Guštāsp, associated together with the divine name of Anāhitā, bring to mind the Vedic *Aśvinau*, the twin gods, often associated with a goddess, and whose name contains *aśva*, "horse." Luhrāsp is only a pale, impersonal, and inactive doublet of Guštāsp, just as the two Aśvins are represented in the Vedic tradition as having exactly the same attributes and functions. The equal span of their reigns is another expression of this twin identity. One recognizes here solutions applied to the difficult problem which could not fail to arise from the conversion of mythical types into historical figures. The same difficulty was resolved in a similar manner in the case of the sacred fire traditionally attached to the cult of the twins: the

Ādhur Burzīn, founded by Luhrāsp, and the Ādhur Mihr Burzīn, founded by Guštāsp, are clearly only an artificial reduplication of the name of the sacred fire of the third estate; in line with a no longer systematic and simultaneous, but chronological and successive presentation of the fires, the name of this fire was repeated with a slight variation, and from it were drawn two fires, as two kings were drawn from the divine twins. And as the great goddess and the divine twins are intimately connected, the cult of fire—and its capital—were located at Balch, where Anāhitā had an important cult center.

Wikander then underlines how these data, in light of what we know of Indo-European trifunctional ideology and its theological and mythological expressions, take on a coherent sense:[4]

> If the Iranian tripartition is identical with the richer and more complex tripartition of the Indo-Europeans, this last section of Iranian legendary history becomes intelligible. Better yet: to a large extent it appears as a coherent statement of this entire conceptual entity. Three points in particular are clarified:
>
> (1) The connection between the fire of the third estate and the mythology of the divine twins is necessary, a result all the more remarkable because Iran no longer preserves the Dioscuric mythology per se.
>
> (2) Equally natural is the increasing role that women play in this section, and not only Nāhīd-Anāhitā, who belongs to the mythology of the Dioscuri, but the queen Humāy (already in the *Avesta*, Humāyā is associated with Vištāspa in the cult of feminine divinities)—this fact is only the epic reflection of the mythological fact that the best characterized goddesses belong on the level of the third function.
>
> (3) The contrast between the new dynasty and the preceding period is not only a matter of the distinction between the second and the third functions, but of a more profound distinction that jointly opposes the first two functions to the third. Thus the Iranian nobles' opposition to Luhrāsp's rise to royal power is, on the epic level, what Indra's opposition to

[4] Ibid., p. 320.

the admission of the Aśvins to the soma-sacrifice is on the mythical plane. In defense of his unexpected choice, Kai Xosrau stresses that Luhrāsp is also of royal origin, because he descends from King Hošang: in ritual terms this means that the Atur Burzēn Mihr, the fire of the third estate, is equal to the others, since it was instituted like the rest by Hošang, as stated explicitly by the religious tradition.

So much corroborative evidence leads one to believe that, up to "the elder Dārā" (Dārāb) in whom is condensed the entire golden age of the Achaemenian empire, real history, assuming that there was such a history here, has been rethought, recast in the mold of the three functions, which provided it with three great natural divisions, with the type of events that occur in each one. Clearly, this is quite a different treatment from the one that in India, within a wider dualistic framework, gave birth to the team of the five Pāṇḍavas—the just king, the two warriors, and the obliging twins. It is no longer a question of one simultaneous picture of the functions, emphasizing the harmonious collaboration of their specialties in a common action, but of a succession of pictures, emphasizing their differences. I have compared it to the successive appearance of the functions, or parts of functions, in the beginning of Roman "history": in the reigns of Romulus and Numa, founders diversely religious and associated with Jupiter; of Tullus Hostilius, strictly and aggressively a warrior; and of the complex Ancus Marcius, under whom the bases of economic power and prosperity are laid down.[5] I have also compared it to the series of first reigns in the history of the Skjöldungar, that of the founder Scioldus, patterned after the great historical Valdemars, organizers and legislators of the kingdom of Denmark; that of Gram, copied from the god Thor; then those of Hadingus and Frotho, based on the two great Vanir gods, Njörðr and Freyr, respectively.[6] Alwyn and Brinley Rees have also suggested interpreting according to this

[5] *Mythe et Épopée* I (Paris, 1968; 2d ed. 1974): 271–274; *The Destiny of the Warrior*, pp. 6–9.

[6] *From Myth to Fiction* (Chicago, 1973), appendix 2.

model the characters ascribed to the successive inhabitants of Ireland, in the epic systematization of the *Book of Conquests*.[7]

The list of the kings, ancestors of the heroes of the *Mahābhārata*, follows a different pattern. It has no value in itself and no structure of its own. It is intended only to usher in or to pave the way for the Pāṇḍavas with a dynastic history as glamorous and opulent as possible; for here as always, and despite the relative brevity of the exposé, India saw things on a grand scale. The genealogy of the Pāṇḍavas is made up of: (1) a small number of famous and colorful entries spaced out through the list, about whom tradition has plenty to say, and several of whom are interchangeable eponyms of the race as a whole (the Pāṇḍavas and their cousins are called Bhāratas and Kauravas, as well as Pauravas, after Bharata, Kuru, and Pūru); (2) a great number of filler entries that are mere names and numbers, and whose only role seems to be to extend the list, to attach a more impressive time span to the dynasty. Many of these "empty terms" also borrow their names from the later "substantive terms," or even from the heroes who will figure in the events of the poem. Thus between Kuru and Śāntanu, Pāṇḍu's grandfather, one of the variants interpolates six terms, including a Parikṣit and a Bhīmasena; Parikṣit will be, at the end of the *Mahābhārata*, the name of the restorer of the dynasty, and Bhīmasena is another name for Bhīma, the second of the five Pāṇḍavas. In the same interval between Kuru and Śāntanu another variant inserts only three terms, including a Janamejaya, then a Dhṛtarāṣṭra who already has as one of his seven brothers a Pāṇḍu; Janamejaya will be the name of the son and successor of Parikṣit in the *post-bharatica*, and Pāṇḍu and Dhṛtarāṣṭra, as nominal grandsons of Śāntanu, are the nominal father and uncle of the Pāṇḍavas.

We have been discussing variants. In fact, following a procedure of which there are many other examples, the poets of the *Mahābhārata* have juxtaposed, in two adjoining sections of the introduction (I, 94 and 95), two genealogies whose "empty terms"

[7] *Celtic Heritage* (London, 1961), pp. 108–117.

differ considerably in three passages, the second one being even more heavily and elaborately laden than the first; but in both texts the "substantive terms" are the same, and appear in the same sequence. From eponym to eponym, the family tree is as follows:

I. Naturally the genealogy goes back to the gods themselves, and to the most abstract ones. Here is this beginning, down to the father of the first eponym, Pūru, in the list of I, 94 (that of I, 95 is the same, but it begins only with Vivasvat):

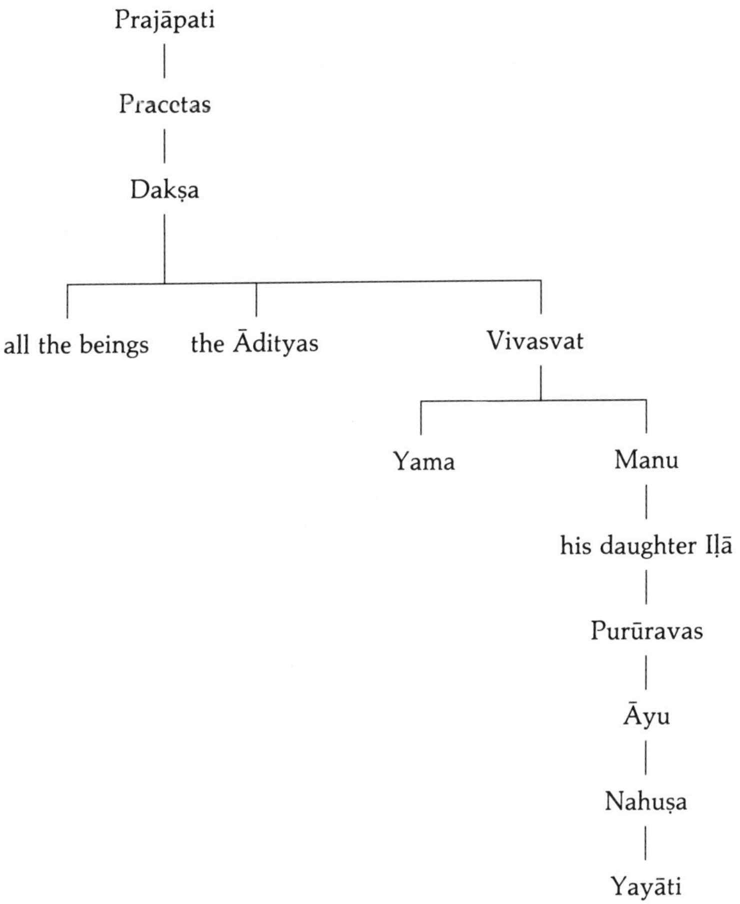

Beginning with Purūravas, all the terms are "substantive," that is, they have personalities and adventures. The posterity of Yayāti is complex, coming from two marriages:

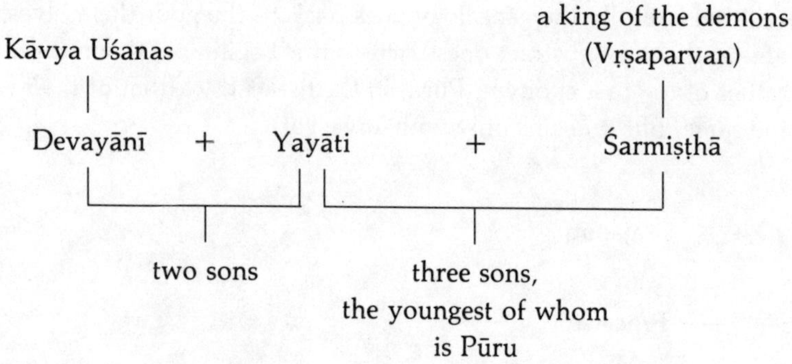

II. After Pūru and in his line, the first "substantive terms" encountered are Duḥṣanta, the forgotten husband of Śakuntalā, and their son Bharata, the second eponym. Between Pūru and Duḥṣanta, the list in I, 94 inserts five "empty terms," the one in I, 95 many more, seventeen.

III. Between Bharata and, in his line, Saṃvaraṇa, the father of Kuru, who is the third eponym, there are four "empty terms" in I, 94, five in I, 95. Kuru is born under the following circumstances:

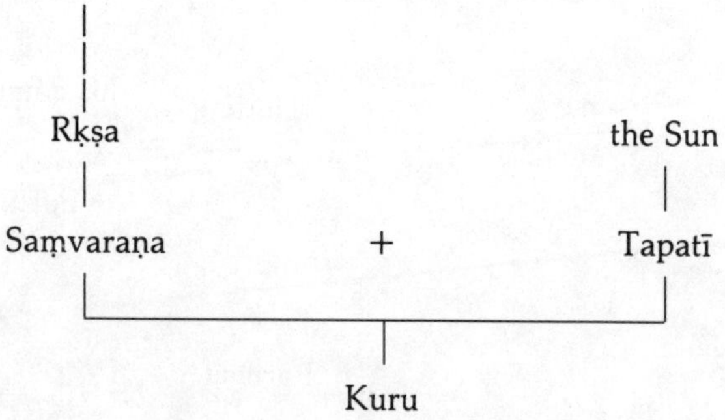

IV. Between Kuru and the first figure who actually belongs to the plot of the poem, Śāntanu, there are three "empty terms" in I, 94 and six in I, 95. The case of Śāntanu and his wives and sons was discussed at length in the first part of *Mythe et Épopée* I; let us recall here the father and his second wife:

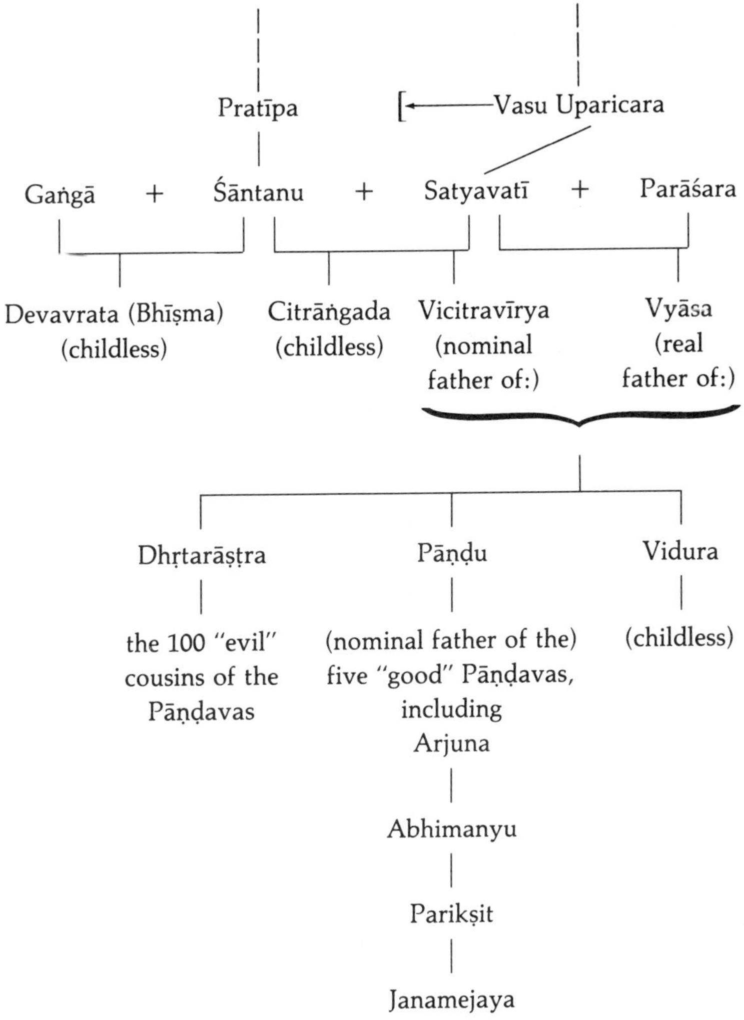

The study that has just been made of Kāvya Uśanas (first table) demonstrates that the "substantive terms" of this long dynasty and those that immediately precede them possibly carry on very old types that Iranian "history," and perhaps other Indo-European literatures, may have used differently.

Thus we have pointed out, if not defined, a wide field for comparative investigations. By way of an example, a separate work[8] has been devoted to one of these figures, one who is certainly important, since he is the father of the first of the three eponyms, and probably ancient, as he is connected as a son-in-law to the mythical, Indo-Iranian Kāvya Uśanas: namely Yayāti (first table), next to whom analysis placed Vasu Uparicara (fourth table).[9]

[8] *The Destiny of a King.*

[9] [1977] This book has moved my friend Stig Wikander not so much to criticism as to an objection, to be found in *Revue de l'histoire des religions* 185 (1974), pp. 3–8, under the title "Épopée et mythologie, examen critique de récentes publications de G. Dumézil." I may have been too brief (here and pp. 10–11 above) in my presentation of Wikander's well-known hypothesis, to which I was won over long ago, on the fundamental identity in subject matter of the Indian and Iranian epics and the structure of the *Shāh Nāmeh*. It is unfortunate that he has not published his *Haskell Lectures* of 1967 (see, ibid., p. 6)—when I succeeded him in the same honor in 1968, *verba*, alas, *volaverunt*. The two lectures whose texts he has subsequently shared with me are full of important new elements.

Wikander has also called my attention to an old article by Hyacinthe de Charencey, "Djemshid et Quetzalcoatl," *Revue des Traditions Populaires* 8 (1893): 241–247. As always, this curious benefactor of oriental studies leaps precariously among the rocks and rapids of ingeniousness, but he provides food for thought.

Designer: UC Press Staff
Compositor: Freedmen's Organization
Printer: Edwards Bros., Inc.
Binder: Edwards Bros., Inc.
Text: 10/13 Paladium
Display: Paladium